# A TRAVELER'S GUIDE TO THE KINGDOM

## JOURNEYING THROUGH THE CHRISTIAN LIFE

✦ ✦ ✦

## JAMES EMERY WHITE

≋
**IVP Books**
An imprint of InterVarsity Press
Downers Grove, Illinois

InterVarsity Press
P.O. Box 1400, Downers Grove, IL 60515-1426
World Wide Web: www.ivpress.com
E-mail: email@ivpress.com

InterVarsity Press® is the book-publishing division of InterVarsity Christian Fellowship/USA®, a movement
of students and faculty active on campus at hundreds of universities, colleges and schools of nursing in the
United States of America, and a member movement of the International Fellowship of Evangelical Students.
For information about local and regional activities, write Public Relations Dept., InterVarsity Christian
Fellowship/USA, 6400 Schroeder Rd., P.O. Box 7895, Madison, WI 53707-7895, or visit the IVCF website at
<www.intervarsity.org>.

All Scripture quotations, unless otherwise indicated, are taken from the Holy Bible, New International
Version®. NIV®. Copyright ©1973, 1978, 1984 by International Bible Society. Used by permission of
Zondervan Publishing House. All rights reserved.

While all stories in this book are true, some names and identifying information in this book have been
changed to protect the privacy of the individuals involved.

The Prayer for the Laying-on of Hands by the Iona Community, quoted on p. 52, is © 2001 The Iona
Community. Taken from The Iona Abbey Worship Book, Wild Publications, Glasgow. Used by permission.

Interior design: Beth Hagenberg
Cover design: Cindy Kiple
Images: Apartheid Museum: © Oliver Gerhard/age footstock
     Photograph of The Eagle and Child Pub: © Stephanie Jenkins
     Photograph of Corrie ten Boom's House: © George Tinsley
     Chartres Cathedral: © Marina Pykhova/Dreamstime.com
     The Wittenberg Door: © Kasparart/Dreamstime.com
     Security Building, Dachau concentration camp: © J. Lang/Shutterstock

ISBN 978-0-8308-3818-9

Printed in the United States of America ∞

Library of Congress Cataloging-in-Publication Data

White, James Emery, 1961-
  A traveler's guide to the kingdom : journeying through the Christian
life / James Emery White.
     p. cm.
  Includes bibliographical references (p.    ).
  ISBN 978-0-8308-3818-9 (pbk. : alk. paper)
  1. Christian pilgrims and pilgrimages. 2. Christian
life—Miscellanea. 3. Christianity—Essence, genius,
nature—Miscellanea. 4. Tourism—Religious aspects—Christianity. 5.
Travel—Religious aspects—Christianity. I. Title.
  BV5067.W45 2012
  263'.042—dc23

2012000267

| P | 18 | 17 | 16 | 15 | 14 | 13 | 12 | 11 | 10 | 9 | 8 | 7 | 6 | 5 | 4 | 3 | 2 | 1 |
|---|----|----|----|----|----|----|----|----|----|---|---|---|---|---|---|---|---|---|
| Y | 27 | 26 | 25 | 24 | 23 | 22 | 21 | 20 | 19 | 18 | 17 | 16 | 15 | 14 | 13 | 12 | | |

# Contents

# A Few Opening Words

I ENVY YOU. I WISH SOMEONE HAD written to me about the things I am going to write to you about. That sounds condescending—like I know a lot that you need to know. That's not what I mean. It's just that my life would have been richer, deeper, saner if someone who had traveled with Christ for many years shared some of those years with me. I may not have agreed with all that was shared, as you will not agree with me, but I would have liked to have listened.

What follows will be a series of reflections, written from various places around the world, which prompted things that seem of importance to pass down. Through it all, I hope to give you a sense of what life in Christ means. Not a life that simply knows *about* Christ, but a life that is *in* Christ. And I want to talk about that with great candor and as much authenticity as I can bring to bear (or bear to bring), because I am sure you are as tired as I am of posture and pretense.

I like these places. They reflect much of who I am. But I also like rooting this particular conversation in place, because place matters. It conveys an emotion; it tells a story; it stands in, and for, history. And history's personalities. As we travel together to pubs and cathedrals, we will immerse ourselves in what God did—and still can do. And perhaps that is what I've always loved most about

traveling; immersing myself in something that might just offer
something back.

Let's pray for that to happen with us.

*    *    *    *

I wish to thank the InterVarsity Press team for their willingness to
see the vision of this book become reality, and particularly my
editor, Cindy Bunch. Special thanks go to Jeff Crosby, whose loyalty and commitment are much-valued.

I continue to be served by my long-time assistant, Ms. Glynn
Goble, and my dedicated writing assistant, Alli Main. Thanks to
you both for your tireless, selfless work on our many projects together.

To my wife, Susan: once again, you have made every page possible.

*Soli Deo gloria.*

# 1

## THE EAGLE AND CHILD PUB OXFORD, ENGLAND

### YOU ARE CONVERTED

*Lewis struck me as the most
thoroughly converted man I ever met.*

WALTER HOOPER, PREFACE TO C. S. LEWIS'S GOD IN THE DOCK

✦ ✦ ✦

Figure 1.1: Ozeye/Wikimedia Commons

I LOVE ENGLAND. I LOVE THE HISTORY. I love the English accent. I love the cabs. I love the double-decker buses and red phone booths. I love the river Thames. I love the quaint little villages. And lest there be any doubt, I love the pubs.

In fact, I want to take you to one tucked away down the street from the center of one of the more well-known cities in England. Oxford. Often called the city of "dreaming spires," Oxford is one of the more beautiful cities on the planet. Its medieval beginnings can still be felt when you walk down cobblestone walkways and through ancient colleges. I have had the good fortune of being able to study there, and still do from time to time through various summer programs. I enjoy any and every hour possible in its famed Bodleian Library, particularly the Radcliffe and Sir Richard Humphrey's library.

But most of all, I return to spend the afternoons writing in my favorite Oxford pub, The Eagle and Child (affectionately known by locals as "The Bird and the Baby"), largely because of who went there before me. As a plaque on the wall reads,

> C. S. Lewis, his brother, W. H. Lewis, J. R. R. Tolkien, Charles Williams and other friends met every Tuesday morning, between the years 1939-1962 in the back room of this their favorite pub. These men, popularly known as the "Inklings," met here to drink beer and to discuss, among other things, the books they were writing.

You will recognize the name of Tolkien as the author of *The Lord of the Rings* trilogy. C. S. Lewis will, hopefully, also be known to you through the movie of his life titled *Shadowlands*, his seven-volume Chronicles of Narnia (also made into movies), as well as such works as *The Screwtape Letters* and *Mere Christianity*. Williams is lesser known to most in our day, but he was greatly respected by the others and was the author of numerous works of fiction. Another frame on the wall contains a note, dated November 3, 1948, which Lewis and others wrote to the owner: "The undersigned, having just partaken of your ham, have drunk your health." This was signed by, among others, Lewis, Tolkien and Tolkien's son Christopher. And drink they did, adding to the lively conversation and the banter that did not let ego gain too much of a foothold, for as one landlady overheard Lewis say to Tolkien, "Oh no, not another bloody elf story to read?"

You would like this pub. The dark interior, the hard wooden floor, the low ceilings, the paneling that travels up half the wall, the network of small rooms, the clink of glasses, the earthy atmosphere, the informal and congenial banter. It speaks volumes that, as something of an introvert, I even enjoy the people in pubs. Every year I find myself in fresh and candid conversations that tend to flow around the tables and over the pints. I recall the very first pub I ever visited during my very first trip to England. I flew into London, and then, due to a speaking engagement, hopped a plane immediately to Manchester. After landing, as I rode in a cab to the hotel, I asked my driver to help me fulfill a long dream by pointing me toward a real, honest-to-goodness, authentic English pub. He didn't even pause. He gave me the name, and told me how to walk to it from where I was staying.

He was right. Few pubs have matched it since. It was filled with men and women, children and, outside, even pets (if you haven't been to one, please get the idea of American "bars" out of your head). It was by a small water channel with long, narrow houseboats moored on its edge. I went to the counter, asked a few questions about the history of the place, and then heard a nearby patron say, "Where are you from?"

Shocked to be addressed by a stranger (like I said, it was my first pub experience), I replied, "The United States."

He rolled his eyes and said, "I know *that!*"

I suddenly realized how much my accent must have stood out.

"North Carolina," I replied.

Someone shouted out, "I've been to Atlanta!"

Another said, "I've got family in Texas!"

A third said, "Is that near Phoenix?"

I knew I was home. It was simply one of the more delightful evenings I have ever spent anywhere.

It has often been said that Starbucks is the American pub in terms of a "third space" after home and work. If so, it is a terribly pale imitation. This is one of the reasons I have taken each and every one of my children not only to the UK, but as they got older, to a night of "pubbing" in London. Not exactly a word, I know, but for us it meant four or five consecutive pubs via the Tube to soak in atmosphere, conversation, food, history and sheer delight.

But back to Oxford. As I sit at my favorite little table just to the side of the small fireplace in the "Rabbit Room" (as the back room where Lewis and friends met is now called), where the smell of wood, coal and tobacco would have been strong in their day, a stream of tourists enter. They gaze at the photographs and memorabilia on the wall, and take their pictures. There is a sense of "this is where it happened" written on their faces. Unfortunately for the owners, they seldom buy a pint.

But what, exactly, happened in this room? What is it about Lewis and his friends that creates such pilgrimages to it? What has made Lewis, in particular, the unofficial patron saint of so many Christians around the world? It wasn't that he filled stadiums with his oratorical skills along the lines of a Billy Graham; the only extant recording of which I'm aware is a snippet of him reading from his book *The Four Loves*. A deep, thoroughly English voice, but nothing one would call charismatic.

One could argue that it was his imagination that gripped us—

Figure 1.2: Tom Murphy VII/Wikimedia Commons

the fantasies of Narnia, the creativity of the letters of Screwtape—and that was certainly a part. But still, such things do not explain the esteem, even the reverence, in which C. S. Lewis is held. Few have been similarly moved to make journeys to the haunts of John Bunyan, author of the most famous work of fiction in Christian history, *Pilgrim's Progress*. And yes, we are taken by Christians who have achieved fame or note in our culture, so whatever intellectual insecurity we might have is certainly bolstered by an Oxford don who *chose* the Christian faith. But Christianity does not lack intellectual adherents. Even the fact that most Americans are closet Anglophiles doesn't quite explain the regard in which we hold Lewis. So what was it about Lewis that has left such an enduring impression on so many?

Unlike the tourists, let's go ahead and purchase at least some fish and chips (I'll leave whether to have a pint to your discretion) and talk about it, and along the way consider what may be the real attraction of Lewis—that he was simply one of the most *converted* figures in Christendom. And in that conversation, let's talk about our conversion, as well. It really is the foundation of everything.

## A MOST RELUCTANT CONVERT

Clive Staples Lewis was born in Belfast, Ireland. Following World War I, where Lewis served in France and was wounded in 1917, he went to University College, Oxford, where he achieved a rare double first in Classics, an additional first in English and the Chancellor's Prize for academics. He was shortly offered a teaching position at Magdalen (pronounced there as Maudlin) College, Oxford, where he was a fellow and tutor from 1925-1954, and then later at the University of Cambridge as professor of medieval and Renaissance English (1954-1963). In 1931, Lewis came out of atheism into the Christian faith, aided significantly through his friendship with Tolkien (I'll tell you that story in a moment). As he journeyed away from his rejection of any type of God, he flirted with several alternate worldviews before Christianity, most seriously Hinduism, but ended with Jesus.

His first published writing, *The Pilgrim's Regress: An Allegorical Apology for Christianity, Reason and Romanticism,* came out in 1933. There followed a torrent of works, eventually reaching forty titles, the vast majority attempting to put forward Christianity in a very non-Christian world. Among the more widely known are *The Screwtape Letters* (a fictional dialogue between two demons about their human patient on earth), a trilogy of science fiction novels (when the genre was hardly known), a series of BBC addresses that became known as *Mere Christianity,* and the Chronicles of Narnia, a series of seven children's books that are widely heralded as classics of fantasy literature and are currently being made into feature films.

All the more reason to marvel that on that day in the Trinity term of 1929 he "gave in, and admitted that God was God, and knelt and prayed." He confessed he did so as "the most reluctant convert in all of England." Yet his friend and personal secretary, Walter Hooper, once commented that Lewis struck him "as the most thoroughly *converted* man" he had ever met.

## AMAZING GRACE

I know I am writing to you as a Christian, but humor me for a moment about what it means to actually *become* one. You are converted when you accept the Person and work of Christ for your life. By Person, I mean the acceptance that here was God himself in human form. By work, I mean the acceptance of his death on the cross as being in our place and for our sins.

But if we are not careful, this can lead us to make conversion akin to a business transaction. "I agree to grant you the truth of these matters, and you agree to grant me salvation in return." Not only does this denigrate the wild love God revealed in his effort to reach out to us in such a manner, but it also runs the risk of trivializing the nightmare predicament in which our sin had placed us. My fear for many of us is that we will lose the true sense of our state as sinners before a holy God. Without a real sense of moral bankruptcy and guilt, we will never appreciate the gift of salvation and the radical nature of grace. Dietrich Bonhoeffer once lamented the prevalence of "cheap" grace, meaning an embrace of grace without a sense of commitment. My fear is the devaluation of grace through a cheapening of its *need*. This was never a question for Lewis. There was a British conference on comparative religions that brought together experts from all over the world to debate what was unique, if anything, about the Christian faith in relation to other religions. Was it the idea that a god became a man? No, other religions had variations on that one. Even the great Greek myths were about gods appearing in human form. Was it the resurrection? No. The idea of the dead returning to life could be found in many different ideologies. Was it heaven, life after death or an eternal soul? Was it love for your neighbor, good works, care for the poor or homeless? Was it about sin or hell or judgment?

The dialogue went on for some time, until Lewis wandered into the room. He asked what the debate was about, and found out that his colleagues were discussing what Christianity's unique contribution was among the many world religions.

"Oh, that's easy," Jack (as he was known to friends) said. "It's grace."

And after they thought about it, they had to agree.

That this was on the tip of his mind speaks volumes about his internal disposition. His sense of moral decay and need for grace led Lewis to invite Christ into every nook and cranny of his life, embracing the totality of his depravity. As the Dutch politician and theologian Abraham Kuyper had proclaimed in an earlier day, "There is not an inch of any sphere of my life that Christ does not say, 'Mine!'" Lewis would have said, "And gladly I give it!" What else, or who else, was there to give it to? Even further, his holistic need for salvation demanded that every inch be given. Simply put, Lewis sought to love God with his heart, soul, mind and strength—and his neighbor, too. This, Jesus said, was everything the law envisioned and contained. But even more, such fulsome conversion is what enabled all of Lewis's gifts to roam free and large. And will allow yours as well.

So let's take Jesus' admonishment at face value. If we are to be converted, and our conversion is meant to be complete—if we are called to love him with heart, soul, mind and strength—then what, exactly, does that mean?

## HEART

Let's begin with our heart. To the ancient Hebrew mind, the heart was the seat of the will. It was the place from which you took charge of your emotions. When decisions were made, directions were taken, purposes were forged, commitments were birthed, allegiances were given, it was always an affair of the heart. This is why in the beatitudes Jesus would say, "Blessed are the pure in heart," for it was there that purity was designed to be in control. And his greatest accusation? "You honor God with your lips, but your hearts are far from him." Why? It is within the depths of our heart that we make our choice for, or against, God.

When Lewis wrote of the awakening of his own heart, he would often describe it in terms of being "surprised by joy." "Joy" for Lewis was the holy grail of life. It was what made the great Norse legends so appealing to him as a boy. Through them he would catch glimpses of something beyond him, transcendent of the human experience, and knew such was the longing of his heart. I am sure you know of the difference between happiness and joy. Happiness is circumstantial; joy is foundational. Happiness has to do with what I feel; joy is who I am. Happiness is cheap; joy is priceless. For Lewis, the joy he longed for *was* God.

If I'm losing you with all this talk of "joy," let me come at it another way. Let's talk about the "whoosh" of life. A pair of philosophers have recently written that in our secular age there is a pervasive sadness. Why? Because the age is secular. There are no shared values, no sense of being determined or created by anything or anyone beyond ourselves. Today, we have to find our own meaning. So what fills the void God once inhabited? *Sports.*

Most of us are too young to remember the emotion that swept through the crowd at Yankee stadium when Lou Gehrig delivered his "Luckiest Man Alive" speech, though it is one of the more popular videos on YouTube. A more contemporary example might be the celebration following the 44th Super Bowl victory by the New Orleans Saints with Drew Brees holding his child during the post-victory celebration. Following on the heels of Hurricane Katrina's devastation, the Saints became America's team, with their improbable victory symbolizing our spirit of resilience.

It is during such magic times that sports are able to provide an experience of intense elevation. This experience has been called "whooshing up." You've felt it; it's like an arena spirituality. You sense it at a concert or a political rally. For Lewis, such things called deeply to him. He hoped for the reality behind the "whoosh." For Lewis, those whooshes were but faint echoes of the real thing. In his autobiography, titled *Surprised by Joy*, Lewis writes "of an unsatisfied desire which is itself more desirable than any other satisfaction. I call it Joy, which is here a technical term and must be sharply distinguished both from Happiness and from Pleasure. Joy (in my sense) has indeed one characteristic, and one only, in common with them; the fact that anyone who has experienced it will want it again."

Glimpses of this joy came to Lewis beside a flowering currant bush on a summer day, stirring the memory of his brother bringing his toy garden into the nursery. And when he read the book *Squirrel Nutkin*. And when he mused over the poetry of Longfellow's *Saga of King Olaf*. In each was a desire, but a desire for what? It was as if the longing of a longing was stirred. Thus began Lewis's journey to God, and when the journey ended, the object of his heart's desire had been found. And in turn, Lewis gave his heart.

The great temptation, of course, is to substitute pale imitations of joy for the real thing. Even as a follower of Christ, we can fall back to the whoosh of experience rather than the source of the whoosh himself. Or as Lewis wrote, "We are half-hearted creatures, fooling around with drink and sex and ambition, when infinite joy is offered us . . . like an ignorant child who wants to go on making mud pies in a slum because he cannot imagine what is meant by the offer of a holiday by the sea. We are," he concludes, "far too easily pleased."

To give of our hearts means to find our heart's desire in God, to be so given and so taken that we seek to do nothing more than immerse our lives in experiencing him as God.

## SOUL

We're also to love the Lord with our souls. The essence of the word *soul* can be found in its root, which literally means "to breathe." When we speak of the soul, we are speaking of the essence of life, the air that fills our lungs. Yet it speaks to more than just being "alive." When we come to the soul, we come to that part of us which is *most* alive, the part of our life which makes us most who we are as persons. There are three foundational dimensions to existence: the physical, the psychosocial and the spiritual. A tree has a physical existence, but nothing more. A whale has both a physical and psychosocial existence, for it is conscious and able to relate in certain ways to other beings. But only we humans have been given a physical, psychosocial and *spiritual* dimension.

It is from this distinction, from our souls, that we gain our identity as sons and daughters of God. When God made you, he put something of himself in you. The soul is that unique element of your life that has been given to you by God that reflects his very image. It is the existence of your soul that allows you to do what only humans can do, which is to respond and relate to God in a personal relationship.

Loving God with your soul begins by entering into a relationship with God by choosing to relate to him. This is what brings you alive through Christ at the soul level. This is followed by soul formation, or spiritual formation, which is the giving over of ever-increasing acreage of your inner world in love and devotion to God, and then allowing him to develop it as he wills. I often think of this as being like a dark cavern that is excavated, opened and then filled with light; in like manner, the soul is to be enlarged and developed and filled with the living God.

The basis of this communion with God is both process and event. Most Christians are arrested in their development because they do not grasp this most single idea—they have had the event, but they have yet to take a step forward on the journey. Indeed, conversion is often *reduced* to an event. But in truth, it is both event and process. This is highly significant, and often talked about in terms of the fact that we *are* saved, we are *being* saved, and we *will* be saved. The fact that you *are* saved refers to your decision to come to Christ as forgiver and leader. That you are *being* saved speaks to the ongoing work of the Holy Spirit to make you increasingly like Christ. And you *will* be saved at the end of time when, standing before God, the verdict on your life will be read and your place in eternity declared at the Great Judgment.

So you live between the two poles of salvation—in the "being" saved part of your spiritual journey. Your eternity is secure, but you are now working that salvation out in and through your life. Yes, it is the work of the Holy Spirit, but your job is to cooperate. The Bible tells us we can resist this work, and can grieve the Spirit relationally. So it is a terribly significant journey. If you are not more like Jesus now than you were a year ago, something is amiss. This is not about perfection, or rising above areas of struggle— simply that there should be *progress*.

Lewis took hold of this aspect of conversion with the utmost earnest, not the least of which was through his ample use of historical mentors—writers who specialized in Christian devotion and spiritual formation and whose writing he devoured. Of the many facts surrounding Lewis's life, it is not widely known that perhaps his primary spiritual mentor was Francis de Sales, a Catholic priest who lived in France and died in 1622 and was later beatified in 1661 by Pope Alexander VII, who later canonized him in 1667. He was made a "Doctor of the Church" in 1877. Lewis once spoke of the "dewy freshness" of de Sales's writing, and there can be little doubt that his water fell on Lewis as a slow summer rain on parched ground. If you read de Sales, and then Lewis, you will see the strong influence in style and substance. You find de Sales explicitly mentioned by Lewis in multiple works, such as *Letters to Malcolm, Letters to an American Lady* and *God in the Dock*. Lewis was not the lone Protestant who allowed himself to be mentored by this spiritual giant; Francis's *Introduction to the Devout Life* was also highly praised by John Wesley. I once spent a year reading Francis's *Introduction to the Devout Life* on my monthly retreats before knowing the formative influence it had on Lewis. It was the similarities between them that drew me to explore the possible connection.

The point is that you have a soul, and it is not meant to be stagnant. It is not a "lump" of something that simply "is." It is your very life—the way you breathe in God. And you need to breathe. And then you need to think.

## MIND

The concept of the mind, or intellect, is not hard for most people to grasp. It refers to the use of our reason and intellectual capabilities to understand the world around us. Jesus went out of his way to make sure that when it came to a comprehensive understanding of our love for God, and hence our conversion, that we would not leave this out. When he answered that the greatest commandment was to love God with all of our heart, soul, mind and strength, he was citing the great "Shema" passage of the Old Testament. Hebrew for "Hear," the "Shema" passage refers to Deuteronomy 6:4-5: "Hear, O Israel: The LORD our God, the LORD is one. Love the LORD your God with all your heart and with all your soul and with all your strength." Interestingly, this command in Deuteronomy ends here.

Jesus went out of his way to add ". . . and mind." A mind for God is terribly important if one is to have a life given to God. As the apostle Paul wrote, the very basis of our spiritual transformation as Christ followers is through the renewing of our minds. Or as the writer of the Proverbs maintained, "as a man thinks in his heart, so is he" (see Proverbs 27:19).

Biblical scholars are often quick to point out the limited relevance of this addition. Most commentaries will airily point out that the four terms, when used in this way, form an idiom that only seeks to demonstrate the comprehensive nature of who we are in light of the call to full devotion. Fair enough, but I'm not convinced that's all there is to it. Jesus was speaking to some very uptight and legalistic Pharisees and Sadducees. The letter of the law—which included quoting the Old Testament Scriptures verbatim—was the test of orthodoxy. So why did Jesus make such a pointed addition to an idiom that already accomplished what he was after? I would argue that at the very least, Jesus wanted to make sure that when anyone thought of giving themselves over to God, they would not forget their mind in the process.

Lewis certainly didn't. The intellectual questions that plagued him during his spiritual journey—why God allows pain and suffering, how Christianity can be the one and only way to God, the place of miracles—became the very questions he navigated with such skill. He sorted out these issues for himself, and then turned around and helped others sort them out as well. Lewis's passion was thoughtfully translating the Christian faith into language that anyone could understand. He was driven to help people know what Christianity was *about*. In a series of radio addresses, given over the BBC during the Second World War but later published in three separate parts, the evidence of his intellectual labors—along with his conversational style, wit, intellect and rough charm—revealed Christianity to millions. The initial invitation was for four fifteen-minute talks. The response was so overwhelming that the BBC gave him a fifth fifteen-minute segment to answer listeners' questions.

Then a second round of talks were requested and given. Lewis's clarity of thought, along with his ability to gather together a wide range of information and simplify it, led one listener to remark after listening that they "were magnificent, unforgettable. Nobody, before or since, has made such an 'impact' in straight talks of this kind." The BBC asked for a third round of talks, this time stretching out for eight consecutive weeks. Lewis consented, but made it clear it would be his last. His goal throughout was simple: "I was . . . writing to expound . . . 'mere' Christianity, which is what it is and was what it was long before I was born."

Eventually compiled in a single work titled *Mere Christianity*, the work continues to make Christianity known to millions. You may have heard of this book. Its appeal rests on two levels: as a first-rate work of apologetics, making a case for the Christian faith; but on a second level, the dynamic inherent within the title. The twentieth century's most accomplished apologist for the Christian faith had little desire to stake out narrow theological ground. He wanted to map out a vast territory on which individuals could gather. Rather than being less intellectual, in many ways, it was more. It was scholarship, not academics, and scholarship is always more winsome and compelling.

If you are like me, you probably desire "mere Christianity." It was a phrase first coined by the seventeenth-century Anglican writer Richard Baxter. Baxter lived through the English Civil War and, as a Puritan, threw his support behind Oliver Cromwell and the Parliamentary forces. It was Cromwell who summoned Baxter from his church in Kidderminster, Worcestershire, to help establish the "fundamentals of religion" for the new government. Baxter complied, but Cromwell complained that Baxter's summary of

Christianity could be affirmed by a Papist. "So much the better," replied Baxter.

As Alan Jacobs writes in his exceptional biography of Lewis, Baxter's challenge was his refusal to allow Christianity to succumb to the spirit of fashion and sect. He was convinced that there was a core of orthodox Christianity that Puritans, Anglicans and Catholics all affirmed and that should have been a source of peace among them. "Must you know what Sect or Party I am of?" he wrote in 1680. "I am against all Sects and dividing Parties: but if any will call Mere Christian by the name of a Party . . . I am of that Party which is so against Parties. . . . I am a CHRISTIAN, a MERE CHRISTIAN, of no other religion." As Jacobs writes, "If the danger in Baxter's time had been warfare among various kinds of Christians, the danger in Lewis's time was the evaporation of Christianity altogether. Yet Lewis felt that the remedy for the first crisis was also the remedy for the second: if Christianity is embattled and declining, it is all the more important for Christians to put their differences aside and join to sing the One Hymn of the One Church."

Mere Christianity is not a reduction of orthodoxy—truth on the lowest level, as it were—but the distillation of Christianity so that it is fermented to its fullest potency. It is the essence of Christianity, stripped of all matters unrelated to its pulsating energy. Fill your mind with this—particularly when you maintain the responsibility of such knowledge—and your conversion will run wild and free. And hopefully, strong.

## STRENGTH

When you think of strength, you obviously think of being strong: exuding physical prowess, going to the gym and seeing what you can max out on with the bench press, building up the stamina for a half marathon. Strength is something easily measured, which is why the relationship between our actions and conversion has been the most obvious and easily tested. The idea is that if you are converted, you'll act in a certain way. And then we fill in the blank about what we mean by "certain way," and the implications of conversion become very neat and tidy. Almost comforting. "Look what I just did," we tell ourselves and God, and confidently assume a gaze of approval.

In many ways this is, of course, true. Nietzsche once said that the only philosophy of any worth was one that could actually be lived. Christianity would tweak that a bit, and say that the only good philosophy is one that *should* be lived. But it is in that "living" that you may find yourself tripped up, and on two fronts. First, through legalism—expectations and rules, guidelines and cultural mores. Fulfilling such things is relatively easy, if you go the way of the Pharisees—meaning externally conforming while inwardly putrefying. But we can be tripped up in a second way. If a converted life is simply moral conformity, well, none of us conform, as we sin with great regularity. So it would seem we either embrace a pseudospirituality or a false one.

A good dose of Lewis is healthy here. While thoroughly converted, he didn't act the way Christians are (many would say) supposed to act. It has often been suggested that he could not even be hired by the evangelical college that now stewards his personal letters due to his pipe-smoking, ale-drinking, free-speaking ways. Do you remember what the plaque at The Eagle and Child said they would do when they met at the pub? *Drink beer.* And do you know when they often met? In the *morning.* In my many hours at The Eagle and Child pub, over many years, I have had conversations with folk who knew Lewis. I have heard tales of how he would often come to class with alcohol on his breath, and sometimes with a bit of what we might call a "buzz." No, not drunk, but without a doubt having imbibed. I was told that he had holes in his coat pockets from where the ashes from his pipe burned through after being inserted inside. He was also widely known to be loud and somewhat earthy in his stories.

There can be little doubt that morality matters. Despite our sinful failings, we are called to lead holy lives where the Holy Spirit is allowed to make us increasingly look like, and act like, Jesus. But this transformation is meant to occur from the inside-out—rather than from the outside-in, following a list of prescriptions that often have more to do with cultural sensibilities than biblical truth.

All that to say, turn your attention to the fruit of the Spirit. Have nothing to do with those who expand it beyond this, and even less to do with those who would not wrestle with the challenge such fruit entails. The fruits of the Spirit are given in nine attributes that demonstrate God's hold on your life in tangible ways. You will hear people argue over what it means to be "Spirit-filled." It's a fruitless argument (sorry—couldn't help the pun), as we have already been told: love, joy, peace, patience, kindness, goodness, faithfulness, gentleness and self-control (Galatians 5:22-23).

This brings to mind another pub story. One day, as I sat at my favorite little table, and another stream of tourists entered—and left—I heard the manager muttering, "Bloody Christians." I was enough of a regular to feel comfortable asking him what he meant.

"Take a look at this," he said, holding up a menu.

"They cost me two pounds each. Two pounds! I ordered hundreds of them, and now I only have ten because they keep getting nicked."

"You mean people are stealing them?" I asked incredulously.

"Yeah, the bloody Christians take the menus, while the bloody students take the spoons and ashtrays."

Understanding students' obvious need for utensils, I couldn't help but ask, "Why the menus?"

"I don't know, it's what they can get their hands on, I suppose," he answered. "It got so bad I started making copies of the menu that they could take—for free—but they still take the good ones."

"I'm surprised they don't try and take what's on the walls, then," I mused, looking at the pictures, plaque, and particularly the framed handwritten letter from Lewis, Tolkien and others commemorating the day they had drunk to the barmaid's health.

"Oh, those aren't real," he said, "just copies. They still get taken. I'd never put the real ones up."

He paused a moment, and then said, "What gets me is that all these people who come in for Lewis are supposed to be Christians, right?"

*Yes,* I thought to myself, *they are.*

The irony is bitter; the manager of The Eagle and Child pub holds Christians and, one would surmise, Christianity itself, in disdain because of the behavior of the Christians who flock to pay homage to Lewis. Many wouldn't dare drink a pint, but they will gladly steal. As Lewis knew, loving Christ with your strength may have less to do with avoiding the beer, and more to do with goodness.

## This Story Is True

Let's leave the pub and take a walk. Just down the street back toward the university, then a left toward the bridge. There, just before the bridge, is Magdalen College. We'll walk past the porter, through the entrance, around the chapel building and through the quad. There we will find Addison's Walk.

The path runs beside several streams of the River Cherwell with an entrance just beside the "New Building" where Lewis had his rooms. By "new," the Oxford loyal refer to the fact that they were

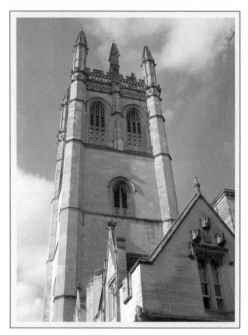

Figure 1.3: Alexis O'Connor/Wikimedia Commons

built in the relatively recent year of 1733. During my summers, I take evening walks there on a regular basis. It has become quite special to me. Let me tell you why.

On Saturday, September 19, 1931, Lewis invited two friends to dine with him in his rooms at Magdalen, where he also taught. One was a man by the name of Hugo Dyson, a lecturer in English literature at Reading University. The other was J. R. R. Tolkien.

On that fall evening, after they had dined, Lewis took his guests on a walk through the Magdalen grounds, ending with a stroll down Addison's Walk. It was there they began to discuss the idea of metaphor and myth. Lewis had long appreciated myth. As mentioned, as a boy he had loved the great Norse stories of the dying god Balder, and as a man, grew to love and appreciate the power of myth throughout the history of language and literature. But he didn't *believe* in them. Beautiful and moving though they might be, they were, he concluded, ultimately untrue. As he expressed to Tolkien, myths are "lies and therefore worthless, even though breathed through silver."

"No," said Tolkien. "They are not lies."

Later, Lewis recalled that at the moment Tolkien uttered those

Figure 1.4: Miles Underwood/Wikimedia Commons

words, "a rush of wind . . . came so suddenly on the still, warm evening and sent so many leaves pattering down that we thought it was raining. We held our breath."

Tolkien's point was that the great myths might just reflect a splintered fragment of the true light. Within the myth, there was something of eternal truth. They talked on, and Lewis became convinced by the force of Tolkien's argument. They returned to Lewis's rooms on Staircase III of the New Building. Once there, they turned their conversation to Christianity. Here Tolkien argued the poet who invented the story was none other than God himself, and the images he used were real men and women and actual history.

Lewis was floored. "Do you mean," he asked, "that the death and resurrection of Christ is the old 'dying God' story all over again?"

Yes, Tolkien answered, except that here is a *real* dying God, with a precise location in history and definite historical consequences. The old myth has become fact. Such joining of faith and intellect had never occurred to Lewis.

It was now 3 a.m., and Tolkien had to go home. Lewis and Dyson escorted him down the stairs. They crossed the quadrangle and let him out by the little postern gate on Magdalen Bridge. Lewis remembered that "Dyson and I found more to say to one another, strolling up and down the cloister of New Building, so that we did not get to bed till 4."

Twelve days later Lewis wrote to his close boyhood friend Arthur Greeves: "I have just passed on from believing in God to definitely believing in Christ—in Christianity. I will try to explain this another time. My long night talk with Dyson and Tolkien had a good deal to do with it."

And so, one man's conversion happened . . . and had also just begun. One that would envelop every inch of his life—head, heart, soul and strength. As should ours.

# 2

# IONA ABBEY
# IONA, SCOTLAND

## YOU ARE SPIRITUAL

*That man is little to be envied,*
*whose patriotism would not gain force*
*upon the plain of Marathon,*
*or whose piety would not grow warmer*
*among the ruins of Iona.*

DR. SAMUEL JOHNSON, OCTOBER 1773

✦ ✦ ✦

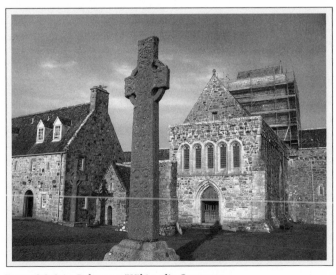

Figure 2.1: Iona Robertson/Wikimedia Commons

I WAS WHIPPING THROUGH CHANNELS on the radio one night as I was driving home from a long and tiring day when I came upon one of the most beautiful songs I had ever heard. It had a different feel than most music, with tin whistles and guitars and mandolins and accordions, and certainly a vocal with a different accent. Its name was "The Valley of Strathmore," and it was performed by the Scottish band Silly Wizard. When the soothing, lovely voice of a young woman named Fiona Ritchie came on the air, I learned I was listening to *Thistle and Shamrock*, a syndicated radio show which specialized in Celtic music. I've never been the same since.

Celtic music led me to Celtic history, Celtic history led me to Celtic spirituality, and Celtic spirituality led me to Celtic pilgrimages: the rocky crags of Skellig Michael rising seven hundred feet out of the North Atlantic off the coast of Ireland; the Holy Island of Lindisfarne rising out of the North Sea off the Northumberland coast of England. The most important was to Iona. I want you to take that particular pilgrimage with me.

The five-hour drive from Glasgow to the Isle of Iona, off the western coast of Scotland, is one of the most breathtakingly beautiful trips you will ever experience. Driving past Loch Lomond and into the highlands, before cutting west to the coast via ferries and one-lane roads, will bring you face-to-face with explosions of mountains marked by countless waterfalls pouring off their sides, cascading into valleys of vivid green. When you come to the He brides, you see that green run straight into the bright blue of the sea—no transition, no melting into each other—just side by side in stark, beautiful contrast, leading to countless islands built of jutting rock serving as tiny sanctuaries of land and hill.

As I boarded the ferry for the final leg of my journey, a short cross over the water with Iona and its medieval ruins in full view, it was as if I were crossing over into another world. I felt a kinship to the place, as I did when I first stepped out on to the moors of

England. Indeed, the two places do not seem dissimilar. Both separate you from the world. As the famed composer Mendelssohn described his visit to Iona in 1829, it is "the loneliest loneliness in the world." The sky envelops you, the wind runs wild and free, and you are thrust before God and God alone.

I have traveled to many places that seemed "spiritual." I have never been quite sure whether it was because it was steeped in religious history, full of mystery, or whether my soul simply resonated with the atmosphere. All I know is that Iona is, for me, a spiritual place. It feels like you are standing on the edge of the world, alone with your spirit before the Spirit, in nature's great monastery where buildings are only a part of the cloister. But why is this small island, only three miles long and half as wide, set apart from all others for pilgrims such as us? Because of one man, and the community he unleashed. Columba came to Iona from Ireland in 563. Although related to one of the ruling families of Ireland, Columba left his native land and founded the famed monastery of Iona. You may have heard how the Irish saved the civilized world by preserving what was lost from the fall of Rome. If so, you can thank Thomas Cahill who came out with the provocatively titled book *How the Irish Saved Civilization.* "Ireland," contended Cahill,

> had one moment of unblemished glory . . . as the Roman Empire fell, as all through Europe matted, unwashed barbarians descended on the Roman cities, looting artifacts and burning books, the Irish, who were just learning to read and write, took up the great labor of copying all of Western literature.

Then missionary-minded Irish monks brought what had been preserved on their isolated island back to the continent, refounding European civilization.

Columba was the heart of the landing. And what a landing. Columba brought Christianity to much of Britain, and according to Adomnan's *Life of St. Columba*—written by Adomnan, the ninth abbot, on Iona before his death in 704—was purported to work such miracles as calming storms and raising the dead. Columba even gave witness to the Loch Ness Monster (which, Adomnan's account relays, he also prevented from attacking one of his companions). By the time of Columba's death, sixty monastic communities had been founded throughout Scotland. It is said that Columba left Ireland for Iona to make penance for a conflict he felt responsible for instigating that resulted in over three thousand deaths, with the hopes of reaching an equal number for Christ. He succeeded.

After Columba's death, pilgrims made their way to Iona, specifically to visit the shrine of Columba, which can still be entered to this day: a little stone building just to the side of the west door of the restored abbey. They would also come to see the large standing crosses, now iconic to Celtic Christianity, with their deep engravings carved into the stone and the circle around the arms. The crosses actually marked the path to the shrine, with the oldest and most famous of them all, St. John's cross, just outside the entrance.

Figure 2.2: Kweedado2/Wikimedia Commons

Columba and his heirs labored from their stronghold on Iona until repeated Viking raids made the treasures of their island too vulnerable to loss. They bought land in Kells, Ireland, and moved their locus of activity there. Yes, the famed "Book of Kells," so associated with Ireland, is actually believed to have been created on Iona. After Columba's spiritual descendants left in the 800s, the abbey fell into disuse until a Benedictine abbey and Augustinian nunnery were established there in 1203. Though built on the site, little of Columba's original church was able to be preserved. This, too, fell into disuse after the Reformation.

Yet pilgrims continue to make the trek to Iona, seeking a sense of spirituality, along with a connection to a vast history of worshiping saints. The island lends itself to that, not least of which through its restored twelfth-century St. Oran's Chapel and the nearby ruins of a similarly aged nunnery. Because of Iona's place in Celtic Christianity, centuries of kings are buried on its grounds, including the famed Duncan and his murderer, Macbeth. You can still see the medieval "Street of Death" that leads from the ferry landing to the abbey where bodies would be carried to their final place of rest. An ecumenical community was founded in 1938 by George Macleod which sought to restore the abbey and reestablish an ongoing worshiping community within its walls, which exists to this day.

When I first went to Iona, I did not know what meaning it would hold for me. I suspected that it would remind me of my affection for the earthy and physical nature of Celtic spirituality. I had a sense that I would resonate with the deep history and ancient nature of the place, particularly its vestiges of medieval life. All this turned out to be true, but there was something more.

Deeply rooted within Celtic spirituality are what are known as "thin places." The Celts believed that the other (spiritual) world was always close to us, but that it was at these places that the veil between the two worlds—the material and the spiritual—was lifted. Islands were particularly noted for their "thin" nature. "Delightful I think it to be in the bosom of an isle on the crest of a rock, that I may see often the calm of the sea," Columba wrote. "That I may see its heavy waves over the glittering ocean as they chant a melody to their Father on their eternal course."

Iona is, to me, a "thin" place. And as the symbol of Celtic spirituality to this day, it should be. Avoiding pantheism (the idea that God *is* everything), as well as panentheism (the belief that God is *in* everything), the ancient Christian Celts saw God *through* everything. The reality of God's immanence ran strong and deep within their spirits. A deep awareness of God's presence informed their daily life to such a degree that any moment, and any task, could become the time and place for an encounter with the living God. They simply assumed that God was present, and lived accordingly. Iona brings that presence to bear on all who land on its shores.

After checking into the small inn, one of only two on the island, I would recall the simple but compelling nature of faith the Christian Celts embraced. Consider the daily task of rising and starting their fire. The act would be accompanied by the following prayer,

> I will kindle my fire this morning
> In presence of the holy angels of heaven.

Then, throughout the day, with every endeavor—from the milking of the cow to the cooking of a meal—the presence of God would be recognized. At the end of the day, when the fire was banked for the night, the last prayerful recognition of God's immanence would be offered:

> The sacred Three
> To save,

To shield,
To surround
The hearth,
The house,
The household,
This eve,
This night,
Oh! this eve,
This night,
And every night,
Each single night.
Amen.

To the Celtic soul, God could be seen as revealing himself in every occurrence of life. John Scotus Eriugena (810–877), arguably the greatest thinker the Celtic church produced, liked to speak of the world as God's theophany (the visible appearance or manifestation of God). And this presence, perceived and looked for in everyday life, was deeply personal.

This was the lesson of the Celtic soul: *they opened themselves fully to God.* But this was no passive quietism. Iona was the beachhead on which Christianity came to Scotland and Northern England. Yes, Augustine came to Canterbury a few years later, and St. Ninian before either of them, but Columba was the real evangelist. Under his leadership, Iona was never some cloistered community that retreated from the world to contemplate and pray. It was the fortress from which Christianity would assail the world. The contemplation and prayer were the spiritual calisthenics that developed a muscular approach to mission. This raises a significant issue; it is only a spiritually transformed life that will transform the world. Put another way, if you wish your one and only life to be active in the world, then Christ must be active in you.

## Spiritual Life

Let's begin at the beginning, which is that you don't actually have a spiritual life. You just have life, and it's meant to be lived spiritually. This is the heart of the matter—are you in a *relationship* with God through Christ? And if so, is it a *close* one? One that is nurtured, cultivated and intimate? If you are not attending to yourself spiritually, your symptoms will be apparent:

- If someone were to ask you where you are growing spiritually, or what new things you are discovering about God, you would not have a ready answer.

- You do not feel close to God; he is more concept than friend, more idea than Father. You are comfortable talking about him as an idea or theological category, but not about your relationship with him.

- You do not often consider God's presence throughout the day.

- You have little or no reserves for crisis moments, such as failure, humiliation, suffering, the death of a loved one or loneliness.

- You publicly worship God, but cannot remember the last time you privately worshiped God.

- You do not feel particularly troubled or convicted by behaviors and attitudes that you know to be sin. You ask for forgiveness, but aren't particularly interested in repentance.

- You would not be comfortable spending time alone with Christ in prayer, or waiting on him to speak to you in a time of silence or solitude.

- You cannot cite the last time you felt a specific prompting come to you from God to act in a counterintuitive way as a result of time spent alone with him. Much less the last time you obeyed such a prompting.

- If someone were to ask you if you were more like Jesus today than you were a year ago, your honest answer would be no.

I don't raise these questions to demean or demoralize, but to awaken you from any spiritual slumber you may have allowed yourself to drift into. Living on the surface of life is easy; days are easily filled with activity and noise, deadlines and duty. Your spirit is beneath the surface, and does not often cry out for attention. The ancient Celts knew that life has to be lived on both levels, and that they had to be brought into union with each other. Jesus certainly felt this need: "Remain in me, and I will remain in you. For a branch cannot produce fruit if it is severed from the vine, and you cannot be fruitful unless you remain in me. Yes, I am the vine; you are the branches. Those who remain in me, and I in them, will produce much fruit. For apart from me you can do nothing" (John 15:4-5 NLT).

So how do you stay connected to Jesus? How do you maintain that union, that intimacy, that relationship? Because it doesn't just happen. Being a Christian does not automatically translate into being close to Christ. I can cross the line into marriage and be, officially, married. But that doesn't mean it's going to be a growing marriage, a close marriage or even a good marriage.

I mentioned that the "Book of Kells" was probably created at Iona before its removal to Kells, Ireland, in the early ninth century in order to be protected from Viking raids. The ornate and highly intricate drawings bringing the four Gospels written in Latin to life reveal the nature of spiritual life so keenly felt by Columba and his descendants. The Gospels are meant to be illustrated—but by our lives.

## THE MYTHS OF THE SPIRITUAL LIFE
Many retreat to Iona for spiritual rejuvenation. But spirituality does not require a place as much as a state of mind, one where

there is—in the ancient Celtic sense—an "inner attentiveness to God" alone. This is easier said than done. Even among pilgrims to Iona. Drawn to the famed Celtic crosses, I went into a small museum behind the abbey to see some of the original carvings. Opening the door, a light immediately tripped on—along with a woman's shrieking voice, "No! No! Oh, da*n you!"

Nice to see you too.

She then apologized and explained that she had been waiting for the automated lights to turn off so that she could take a flash picture, and my entrance had tripped them back on. She apologized, realizing that she had cursed me over a picture of a cross.

But we all fall into that pit, don't we? We are not very much like Jesus, and often have no idea how to be. We try to capture his life like a photo only to have our actions spew forth obscenities through our failures.

Why is there such a disconnect? Partly because of the myths we believe about the life we are trying to live.

Let's walk around a bit to see if we can talk this through. Iona is not a place to remain indoors—it is a place to seek the convergence of heaven and earth where God breaks in with breathtaking immediacy, bringing truth to bear on our inmost parts.

As we venture into the windswept wildness of the small isle, walking toward the restored abbey and the ruins of the nunnery, I'm reminded of the last stanza of the eighth-century "Deer's Cry," more popularly known as St. Patrick's breastplate, perhaps the greatest of all Celtic hymns:

> Christ with me, Christ before me; Christ behind me, Christ in me; Christ under me, Christ over me; Christ to the right of me, Christ to the left of me; Christ in lying down, Christ in sitting, Christ in rising up; Christ in the heart of everyone that thinks of me; Christ in the mouth of everyone that

speaks to me; Christ in every eye that sees me; Christ in every ear that hears me.

And isn't this what we long for? So let's clear away the barriers, particularly the myths that permeate our thoughts—and our actions.

*The instantaneous myth.* Our first stop, and rightfully so, is St. Columba's Shrine. As mentioned, it's a little stone building just to the left of the west door into the church. Most of the walls were restored in 1962, but the lowest foundations are original and date back to at least the ninth century. The tradition linking the shrine to Columba flows from the preservation of ancient knowledge as to where the saint had first been buried. In order to respect its antiquity and sanctity, the building was left free-standing even after the medieval abbey was constructed. Many believe that the abbey was constructed around the shrine. During certain hours of the day, the shadow of St. John's cross falls across its front.

It is a small space; we stoop to enter. There are small mats and pillows for kneeling. Some candles are lit, barely illuminating the dim interior. We feel an ancient air coupled with a deep sense of the sacred. It would be difficult to imagine more than a few people in here at a time, but then again, it was not a space built for groups. It was a space built for solitary worshipers who made pilgrimages to Colomba's grave in recognition of his life and the life they, too, would devote to becoming more like Christ each day.

And this reveals the first misunderstanding about the nature of the spiritual life; that spirituality happens, instantly, at the moment you enter into a relationship with God. The belief is that when someone gives their life to Christ, there is an immediate, substantive, in-depth miraculous change in habits, attitudes and character. Just add God, and you get a spiritual life! The truth is that entering into a relationship with God does nothing more than begin the development of that relationship. Deep, lasting life change does not often happen at the moment your relationship with God begins. The Holy Spirit can do whatever he wishes, but even the most casual of observers would quickly note that he hasn't desired to do this with frequency.

When you begin your relationship with God, your eternal destiny is altered, there is a radical reorientation of priorities, there is a new life-purpose, and there is the power and work of God in your life. But rather than instant communion with God at the deepest of levels, there is rather the beginning of a new relationship that develops in intimacy over time. And rather than the immediate liberation from every bad habit or character flaw you've ever possessed, what takes place is more like the landing of an army on the beachhead, which then begins routing out the enemy as it makes its way inland. This is why the Bible says, "Let your roots grow down into him and draw up nourishment from him, so you will grow in faith, strong and vigorous in the truth you were taught" (Colossians 2:7 NLT 1996).

Did you catch that language? You have to *let* your roots grow; you have to *draw* up nourishment; you have to *keep on* growing; you have to *become* strong and vigorous. It isn't something that just happens—it's something you have to be intentional about. Becoming a Christian is just the beginning of the journey; it's the *start* of a life that follows Christ. As Richard Foster has written, "Superficiality is the curse of our age. The doctrine of instant satisfaction is a primary spiritual problem. The desperate need today is not for a greater number of intelligent people, or gifted people, but for deep people." Standing in the cloisters of the abbey, imagining the monks of old, you want the spirituality of the place to seep into your being. This is good. We are activists at heart, and think more of "doing" than "being." Indeed, drawing from Celtic sensibilities, there is no such thing as a spiritual journey; if it were, it would "be only a quarter inch long, though many miles deep."

*The time myth.* Let's move on to the abbey, and specifically the cloister. You've seen this design before, I'm sure. In monastic houses throughout western Europe you find the buildings in which the monks lived and worked surrounding a central court or "cloister." They look like four covered walkways, lined with columns, with a quiet courtyard of meticulously groomed grass in the center. The cloister served as a place for quiet prayer and reflection, as well as part of the processional route around the abbey.

Figure 2.3: Used courtesy of Susan Gaddis/www.susangaddis.net.

From the cloister you can enter the chapter house where the monks would meet daily (the original stone bench seats around the walls survive), the day-stair that led up to the monk's dormitory (off the choir area of the abbey is the "night stair" which provided direct access from the monk's dormitory to attend night services), and the undercroft (a cellar or storage room). As a bridge between the daily life and the worshiping life of the monks, the cloister stands as a symbol of the joining of the two levels of life we must live, the two worlds we must inhabit, and perhaps most of all, the two times between which we stand—the now, and the not yet.

Which brings us to the next myth: that true spirituality is merely a by-product of time on earth. The truth is that being a Christian does not automatically translate into *becoming* Christ-*like*. A five-year-old Christian will not necessarily have five years' worth of spiritual maturity. We must intentionally cross through the cloister of life, drinking deeply from the well of Christ, else the worlds—no matter how much intellectually embraced—will remain separate.

Intriguingly, the ancient Celts not only spoke of "thin places," but "thin times." Not all time is created equal, or affords the same spiritual benefits. It is what we do with our time that makes it "thin" or "thick." One lets God in, the other keeps the work of the Spirit at bay.

Since St. Andrews, Scotland, is also the birthplace of the ancient game of golf—documented as a game from at least 1552 and governed in almost every country of the world by the Royal and Ancient Golf Club housed at St. Andrews—perhaps it is a fitting analogy. I first picked up the game of golf when I was in graduate school. I took all of two lessons from a course pro, bought a set of clubs and began to play. Initially, I made excellent progress. But then I began to play with less and less frequency. Soon, I only played at the annual Christmas gathering with my wife's family. As you might expect, I would play about the same each year—translation, horribly—because I hadn't played since the previous year. Recently, I have started to play with more regularity, and my game has improved dramatically. But if someone were to ask me how long I've played, the answer would be deceiving. I could tell them I've played for over two decades, but it wouldn't mean anything, because I haven't been *intentional* about the game over that time. People who have only been playing the game a year, but have developed their game through lessons and practice, could easily outplay me.

This is a crucial understanding. I can subscribe to golf magazines, purchase golf equipment, live by a golf course, wear golf clothing, watch golf on TV and frequent the clubhouse—*and never improve my game!* Simply being exposed to something has little bearing on whether or not we become proficient at it. While your spirituality takes time, it is not simply a *product* of time. As the biblical writer of Hebrews noted to a group of Christians, "though by this time you ought to be teachers, you need someone to teach you the elementary truths of God's word all over again" (Hebrews 5:12).

The heart of Christian spirituality is to be like Jesus. And to be like Jesus you *train.* You do the things Jesus did in order to live like Jesus lived. That's why Jesus once said that "everyone who is *fully trained* will be like his teacher" (Luke 6:40). And the apostle Paul wrote, "*train yourself* to be godly" (1 Timothy 4:7; cf. 1 Corinthians 9:24-26). "Anyone who is not a continual student of Jesus, and who nevertheless reads the great promises of the Bible as if they were for him or her," writes Dallas Willard, "is like someone trying to cash a check on another person's account." The key to a spiritual life is to order your life around those activities, disciplines and practices that were modeled by Christ in order to accomplish through training what you currently cannot do simply through exposure.

That is what Iona offered to those who made their way to its shores. It was a monastic community designed to train spiritual athletes. They retreated to the edge of the world to engage with

Figure 2.4: Torsten Henning/Wikimedia
Commons

God, but then launched themselves from that very edge to engage the world.

*The transformation myth.* One of the most haunting places on Iona is the nunnery, unrestored, lying in ruins, but still among the best preserved in all of Britain. Like their male counterparts in the abbey, the nuns followed a life of contemplation and prayer. We are free to wander among what's left of the stone church and chapel, the cloister yard which was used as a garden, the refectory and kitchen. It is a deeply moving and holy place, and something of a picture of the nature of our lives. We don't need to be "put together" to be offered to Christ, or even begin to bring honor to him. He begins where we are, taking the ruins of our life and filling them with his presence.

This speaks to what is perhaps the greatest myth of all—that to become spiritual, you have to first *be* spiritual. No! It's when you come to God that you begin the process of transformation. The biblical order of events is to come as you are, receive God's gift of a personal relationship and then enter into the transformation process. And even then, it will often be a process of three steps forward, two steps back. This has been called the "law of undulation." To "undulate" means to move in waves, to go "up and down" in terms of your progress. And this is how human beings *are* when it comes to the flow of their spiritual life. It is the nearest thing we humans have to normalcy!

The law of undulation is important to remember, because it is often believed that true spirituality is gauged by *feeling*. Do I *feel* close to God? Do I *feel* spiritual? The reality is that authentic spirituality, while a dynamic enterprise that involves your entire being, has more to do with how you *respond* to your emotions than it does your current emotional state. There will be times you feel up or down, high or low; and in truth, it may have very little to do with the actual state of where you are at with God. The state of your spirituality does not rest on how you feel, but on who you are—and who you are *becoming*. And God is in the soul-making business. He *does* promise to transform you!

This is why the Bible says in Galatians, "Do not hold back the work of the Holy Spirit" (1 Thessalonians 5:19 NCV). And in Ephesians the Bible says, "Let the [Holy] Spirit change your way of thinking and make you into a new person" (Ephesians 4:23-24 CEV). Circle that word *let*! One of the wonders of the Christian life is that God actually takes up residence inside of you. He enters into your inner world, your moral conscience and spirit. That's why Scripture says in Galatians 5, "Let us follow the Holy Spirit's leading in every part of our lives" (Galatians 5:25 LB). God wants to transform you. He wants you to come to him as you are, receive the gift of grace, forgiveness and love, and let him begin the process of molding you and developing you into all that you were created to do and be.

This is the message laden throughout what is arguably the best-known Celtic prayer set to music, one that millions have sung without knowing of its origin. The eighth-century prayer was composed in Old Irish, and began:

Rob tu mo bhoile,
a Comdi cride.
Ni ni nech aile,
acht ri secht nime . . .

It was then offered in a metrical, poetic version and set to a traditional tune named for a hill near Tara where St. Patrick challenged druid priests by lighting a fire for an Easter celebration in open opposition to the edict that only one fire was to burn in the land, and that for the pagan feast of Bealtaine. Now, we sing,

Be thou my vision,
O Lord of my heart;
Naught be all else to me,
Save that Thou art.
Thou my best thought,
by day or by night;
Waking or sleeping,
Thy presence, my light.

"Most of us turned to Christ when we realized there was a difference between Christianity as a religion and Christianity as a relationship," writes Ken Gire. "Sometime after entering into that relationship with Christ, we realized something else. That there is a difference between a personal relationship with Christ and an intimate one." You must cooperate with God's leading and direction in your life, and make the necessary investments to position yourself for his ongoing work in your life, in order to enhance his creative activity. While spirituality consists of being, not doing, there are things to *do* that will help you *be*!

## Quiet Times

Just outside the abbey is a small, freestanding building made of stone known as St. Oran's chapel which was built in the twelfth century. Once inside, you see a tomb-recess, built in the late fifteenth century, perhaps by John, the last Lord of the Isles. St. Oran's Chapel is surrounded by ancient burials in the section known as Reilig Odhrain, with the medieval "Street of Death" passing directly in front of its door. It is open at all times for prayer, with candles lit at the front in what is an otherwise bare space with a stone floor.

When I was in college, there was a small Episcopal chapel made of stone next to our school that was kept open twenty-four hours a day for prayer. A single candle was always lit. It became hallowed ground for me (I even proposed to my wife there). St. Oran's chapel reminds me of that place which held so many quiet times with God. There my relationship with God was forged and given life. Why? It is there I retreated from the world, quieted myself and prayed.

Iona is a naturally quieting place. There are no cars allowed except by permit for the few local residents, and few structures: only an inviting stillness. The mere sight of the abbey—the medieval ruins, the crosses—presses you on every side to turn inward. This is why many come.

But it doesn't take Iona to go there. I'm going to suggest one simple, daily routine. It's no secret that when it comes to relationships there is a direct link between time and intimacy. Your closeness to someone is tied to how much time you spend with them. If you spend five minutes a month with someone, then you're five-minutes-a-month close. If you spend five minutes a day with them, then you're five-minutes-a-day close. I'm much more intimate with someone that I see every day than someone I see once or twice a year. It's no different with God. If you want to develop your relationship with him, you have to spend time with him. And the more time you spend with him, the closer you'll be, and the more your relationship will develop.

Countless numbers of people desiring to develop their spiritual life have invested in a regular, often daily, "quiet time" with God. They've set aside quality time to invest in their relationship with God through prayer and reflection on the Scriptures. They join with the psalmist, who wrote, "Every morning I lay out the pieces of my life on your altar" (Psalm 5:3 *The Message*). So let's examine what this would involve. If you were to take time to be with God, what would you actually *do*?

It begins with solitude and silence. Thomas Kelly talks of the need to go into the "recreating silences." This is the first thing we should allow our quiet times to afford us—quiet. The Celts knew that life is meant to be lived on two levels—the level of activities, and the level of the interior life. The temptation is to live on one level alone. This is why you have to stop long enough to let God speak to you, reveal himself to you, and engage you—and why coupling solitude with silence is so powerful. As Samuel Chadwick once observed, "It would revolutionize the lives of most [people] if they were shut in with God in some secret place for half an hour a day."

But silence and solitude—for its own sake—will not nourish your soul or enliven your intimacy with God. The time must have content, purpose and direction. This is the difference between Christian meditation and many forms of Eastern meditation. For the Buddhist, the goal is to empty the soul. For the Christian, the goal is to *fill* it. We must go from *detachment* to *attachment*. As Dietrich Bonhoeffer once wrote, silence is "nothing else but waiting for God's Word and coming from God's Word with a blessing."

This involves three primary activities: reading the Word of God, reflecting on the Word of God and then responding to the Word of God. *Reading* simply involves using your eyes to take in what is on the surface. *Reflecting* on the Word of God engages your mind to see what is beneath the surface. *Responding* to the Word is giving what we have seen a place to live within our heart. To read the Word without taking time to reflect on it would be like sitting at a table where a sumptuous meal has been prepared and eying all the food but never eating. And to reflect on the Word without prayerfully responding to it would be like chewing the food but never swallowing. The Word of God comes in the "recreating silences," but we must determine whether or not we will let it "recreate" us.

The final component to time with God is prayer. This time of prayer can be guided by many things, not the least of which is your response to the Word from God received through your time *with* the Word, resulting in confession or thanksgiving, praise or request. Ideally, all four of these dynamics will be present as you pray.

The Celts were deeply trinitarian, and not simply in their theology. As Calvin Miller has observed, "They never allowed the Father and the Son and the Spirit to become separate." A typical morning prayer, disarming in its simplicity, would be:

I awake in the name of the Father who made me.
I arise in the name of the Son who died to save me.
I rise to greet the dawn in the name of the Spirit who fills me
    with life.

As the Trinity cannot be separated, nor can the elements of prayer. It is praise, confession, thanksgiving and request. To take one away from the others would be to diminish the fullness of prayer for our life.

While on Iona I went to an evening prayer service where perhaps a hundred or so people were in attendance. (And by the way, if you ever go, stay the night so that you can experience the island after the tourists are gone). It was breathtakingly beautiful;

candlelight played off of the ancient stone of the abbey's long, narrow, vaulted Norman transept. Songs were sung, prayers were offered. We began with praise and then moved to confession, but ended with asking God for healing and help. Name after name was read for prayer, and then those in attendance were invited to come forward and kneel where people laid hands on them and prayed: drug addiction, alcoholism, deserted spouses, financial shortfalls, unemployment, the seeking of God's will, grief over a lost loved one.

With each person, the same prayer was offered:

Spirit of the living God,
present with us now;
Enter you;
body, mind and spirit,
And heal you of all that harms you,
In Jesus' name, Amen.

At the end, the leaders themselves knelt to receive the prayer. It was a beautiful picture of the movements of prayer that should cascade over our life.

## SEVEN MINUTES A DAY

If you're new to this, let me make a suggestion. Start off with just seven minutes. Five minutes is probably too short, and ten minutes may be too long at first, so begin with seven. All of us should be able to manage seven minutes a day with God.

Here's the plan: Set your time; let's say it's first thing in the morning. Know where it is you are going to go. Then set the alarm. When it goes off, get yourself up, make the coffee, grab your Bible, and go to the place you have chosen. Once there, invest the first thirty seconds preparing your heart. Maybe just thank God for a good night's sleep, or for a new day to live. In those thirty seconds, you might want to ask him to open up your heart so that you can be responsive to what he might say to you through prayer or what you read. Ask him to be with you, to meet with you, to speak to you and to teach you. Just thirty seconds.

Then take your Bible and read it for two or three minutes. Just read it. I would suggest that you start reading one of the biographies of Jesus, like Mark. Then take a minute or two and *reflect* on it, including how you might respond. The next day, pick up where you left off. Don't race through your reading, but don't get bogged down either. Read for the joy of reading, and just let God speak to you. Four minutes total.

Each day, after you've spent four minutes reading and reflecting on the Bible, letting God speak to you, spend two and a half minutes in prayer where *you* talk to God. Tell him what's on your mind, ask for his forgiveness, thank him for things he's done, and ask him for what you need, or for the needs of others. Two and a half minutes.

So take thirty seconds preparing your heart and asking for God's presence and guidance; four minutes reading and reflecting on the Bible, listening to his word to you; then two and a half minutes talking to him. Seven minutes a day with God. After a while, you'll discover that seven minutes quickly becomes ten, and then fifteen, and soon you'll be spending the kind of solid, consistent, rich time with God that transforms your life on the deepest levels, and develops the kind of intimacy you've always wanted between you and God.

When she was around five years old, my oldest daughter, Rebecca, would get up early in the morning. When she did, she would get out of her bed, come into Susan's and my bedroom, walk over to my side of the bed, tap me on the shoulder, and whisper, *"Come be with me, Daddy, come be with me."*

I'd usually be asleep, and the last thing I wanted was to get out

of bed, but when I heard that soft little voice, and opened my eyes
to see that precious little girl in her nightgown, wanting to be with
her daddy, I just melted. So I'd get up, and we'd be together—just
the two of us. How could I say no? How can you turn down someone you love, and who loves you and just wants time with you?
Those were priceless times, and they did so much for our relationship. I can't imagine what my life would be like—much less what
my relationship with my daughter would be like—without them.

   I'll tell you what I think. Every morning God comes to the side
of your bed and says, "*Come be with me.*" And if you'll say yes,
you'll be very, very glad.

# 3

## St. Catherine's Monastery Mt. Sinai, Egypt

### YOU CAN BE LED BY GOD

*He is there,*
*and He is not silent.*

Francis A. Schaeffer

✦ ✦ ✦

Figure 3.1: ccarlstead/Wikimedia Commons

AFTER TAKING THE FLIGHT FROM Dubai to Cairo, from Cairo to
Sharm el-Sheikh, and then the two-and-a-half-hour drive into the
barren Sinai desert surrounded by equally barren and rugged
hills, my one thought made me feel guilty: If the Israelites wandered forty years in this, no wonder they grumbled.

But with a destination like St. Catherine's monastery, it was
worth every effort. There is no other place on the planet you can
visit that transports you so far back into redemptive history. For
here we have the place where, second only to the incarnation itself, God made himself most clearly known. First through a burning bush on the side of a mountain, and then later, descending in
power and glory onto the top of the mountain itself, writing his
very law onto stone tablets for humankind.

The construction of St. Catherine's was commissioned by the
Byzantine emperor Justinian in 530, though Christians had been
coming there to escape persecution, or as anchorites in pursuit of
a monastic life, since the 300s. It was built as a result of its prox-
imity to Mt. Sinai, but also to protect Christians in the area and to
protect what is purported to be the bush that drew Moses to his
first encounter with the living God. It is very much like a castle,
with high walls and a fortress-like appearance. Mt. Sinai itself is
just behind the side of the mountain on which St. Catherine's is
built, reached by a winding trail to the left and behind the monastery. The trail to the top is often taken by pilgrims at hours of the
day that allow reaching the top by sunrise or sunset. Local Bedou-
ins eagerly offer camel rides to those less inclined to make the
long walk, particularly the final 3,750 Steps of Repentance carved
by monks.

The famed bush, whether the actual one or not, is certainly
there. It lies within the oldest part of the monastery in a small,
roped-off courtyard at the end of a narrow walkway. Intriguingly,
it appears dead on the bottom, but alive on top. It looks something

like a large hanging plant. I've been told that its age has been determined to be in the hundreds of years, and that no cutting from
it will take root. I won't comment on the bright red fire extin-
guisher in the corner.

The oldest and most sacred part of the monastery is the small
chapel built next to the bush, the Chapel of the Burning Bush,
which dates from the fourth century. It is filled with icons (it is an
Orthodox monastery) and hanging candle lamps with ostrich
eggs on top. I've never seen anything quite like them; they are
truly beautiful. St. Catherine's is also home to an incredible library, closed to the public but second only to the Vatican in terms
of treasures and ancient manuscripts, particularly iconography.
While I was there, I was able to see on display two of its treasures:

the "Christ Pantokrator" from
the first half of the fifth century, which I think you would
recognize if you saw it. It is the
classic picture of Christ that
dominates ancient Christianity
and, to this day, Orthodox
faith.

I also saw part of the *Codex
Sinaiticus,* which dates from the
middle of the fourth century,
among the oldest manuscripts
of the Bible and the source for
modern translations to this day.
The one I viewed is thought to
be one of the fifty sent to Constantine, who likely donated it
to the monastery upon its
founding. The original codex,

Figure 3.2: Polimerek/Wikimedia
Commons

considered at the time to be the only copy, was taken by the Russian entrepreneur Tischendorf in 1844 and 1849 under dubious pretenses through trusting monks, who then sold it to the British Library in London where it remains to this day. Certain folios were found later by the monks, but needless to say, they continue to want their codex back.

You may wonder how St. Catherine's has survived with all of its treasures, particularly as a Christian stronghold in the midst of the heart of Islam. Thank Muhammad himself. The monastery is protected by the "Patent of Mohammed," which Muhammad granted to the monks in 623, giving it rights and privileges in perpetuity. A copy of the patent still hangs prominently in the monastery to this day.

Why do I want to introduce you to St. Catherine's, besides its tie to the deepest of biblical past? It's because St. Catherine's reminds us that there is a God, and he has not been silent. He has been making himself known from the very beginning. Your God *is* the God of Moses. Your God *is* the God of Sinai. Your God *is* the God of the burning bush. Your God *is* the God of everything, and everyone, you read of in the Bible, which means he is the God who desires nothing more than to make himself known. You can hear from God, which means you can be led by God. Living the life you long for, and that God longs for you, depends on it.

## Life from the Desert
So how do you hear from God? As it did with Moses and the Israelites, much of it begins in the desert. If you recall, Moses fled to this arid wasteland after murdering a man. To this day, it is still a good place to go if you want to drop out of circulation for a while. All we are really told about this forty-year interim period of his life is that he got married, had a son and then worked for his father-in-law, Jethro, tending his sheep. That's it—nothing more—until

his encounter with God at the burning bush. But let's read between the lines. In fact, let's read a lot between the lines. Here was a prince who was now living in the desert outback. Where once people bowed low before him as he passed by, now he bends his back in manual labor, perhaps for the first time in his life. And he's indebted: working for his father-in-law, tending his father-in-law's sheep, living on his father-in-law's land.

What happens to someone in that kind of situation? You've probably been in a desert or two yourself, times when there was little to bolster your self-esteem. The desert is a season when you feel emptied of any and all sense of worth, accomplishment or merit. Your ego is parched. It's a strong word, but the desert is the place of *breaking*, when you are broken down in ways that are excruciatingly humbling and often painful. But from the brokenness you are able to hear God with the utmost clarity, because pride and pretense have been silenced.

In this desert, you can, of course, stay deaf. The gifts of the desert are not forced on you. You can choose to become bitter and resentful, and more prideful than ever. Or you can become defeated, with a sense that your life is over. God can't use resentment, and God can't use someone who allows himself or herself to give in to a sense of self-pitying defeat. But he *can* use someone who has been humbled and, as a result, become teachable. Because that is someone who will listen to God speak into their life. This is more important than you might think. It is never a question of whether God will speak and lead; it is whether you will have an openness to his words.

Of course, the "desert" times are more than seasons where our spirits are broken enough to be opened to God; they are also when our spirits are quieted enough to hear him. Only in the desert of silence and solitude can we separate ourselves from the world and its noise and activity and distraction. In the desert we come face to face with our souls, and our souls are confronted by God. As Frederick Buechner once observed, the Bible uses hearing, not seeing, as the predominant image for the way human beings know God. This explains why, according to the desert tradition, the emptiness of the desert was actually quite full; it was out of the deadening silences that one could be reborn.

Little wonder that throughout the biblical record, and then throughout church history, the desert has been the place of God's deepest work on human souls. Here we see Moses in the desert for forty years before the greatest season of his life; we also have Jesus entering into the desert for forty days to prepare for his ministry; and the group of men known as the Desert Fathers came to some of Christianity's deepest and most penetrating insights into life with Christ in its barren lands. As the desert father Abba Antony said, "The man who abides in solitude and is quiet, is delivered from fighting three battles—those of hearing, speech and sight. Then he will have but one battle to fight—the battle of the heart."

## It Starts with a Bush

I could take you to where God told me to marry my wife, Susan; where God told me to give up music and pursue a life of speaking and writing; where God told me to start a church. These were nothing less than shouts from God. What I mean is that he spoke so clearly, so strongly impressed himself and his will on my spirit, it was as if he had thundered from Sinai. There was no doubt in my mind what I was to do. His finger had written it on the tablets of my heart.

God will do that time to time. For Moses, the first of many shouts to his heart from God was a burning bush. The story itself is worth a close look at this point:

Now Moses was tending the flock of Jethro his father-in-law, the priest of Midian, and he led the flock to the far side of the desert and came to Horeb, the mountain of God. There the angel of the LORD appeared to him in flames of fire from within a bush. Moses saw that though the bush was on fire it did not burn up. So Moses thought, "I will go over and see this strange sight—why the bush does not burn up." When the LORD saw that he had gone over to look, God called to him from within the bush, "Moses! Moses!"

And Moses said, "Here I am." (Exodus 3:1-4)

A familiar passage to you, perhaps. But did you notice the chain of events? First, we have Moses doing life the way he had been doing it for years. It was a day like any other, a good reminder that we can seldom anticipate God's communications.

Second, God appeared to him through a burning bush. A strange sight, as it burned without burning up. It wasn't the bush that was significant; it was the fact that God brought something into his life that demanded attention. It could have been a crisis or traumatic event; it could have been a moment of helplessness, or of feeling overwhelmed. Anything that invades your life and demands your attention can be an opening salvo from God.

Third, Moses decided to pay attention to the event. He went over to it, determined to explore what it might hold for his life. This, too, is key. The events in our life are experienced, but few are explored for what

Figure 3.3: Alex-ST16/Wikimedia Commons

they might mean on the deepest levels of who we are and what God might be wanting to say to us.

Fourth (and this is critical), did you notice the following words: "When the LORD saw that he had gone over to look"? God did not speak, nor does it appear that he was going to speak, unless and until Moses approached the bush. When Moses went to look, *then* God spoke. If you want to hear a word from God, a good beginning is to demonstrate your willingness and desire to hear it. I'll never forget reading a challenge from an address given by Norton Sterrett back in 1948 to a group of college students. All he said was, "How many of you who are so interested in finding out the will of God for your life spend even five minutes a day praying for him to show it to you?" And it is precisely that five minutes a day that equates to going over to look at the bush.

A life led by God is a life that hungers for a word from God; it is a life that will be relentless in pursuit of that word. Let me get very specific: how fervently have you prayed? How passionately have you searched the Scriptures? How intently have you sought counsel? How purposefully have you launched out in ways that afford God the opportunity to direct your steps? Hearing a word from God is anything but a passive enterprise.

## It Continues with a Tent

Again, let's return to the story itself:

> Now Moses used to take a tent and pitch it outside the camp some distance away, calling it the "tent of meeting." Anyone inquiring of the LORD would go to the tent of meeting outside the camp. And whenever Moses went out to the tent, all the people rose and stood at the entrances to their tents, watching Moses until he entered the tent. As Moses went into the tent, the pillar of cloud would come down and stay at the

entrance, while the LORD spoke with Moses. Whenever the people saw the pillar of cloud standing at the entrance to the tent, they all stood and worshiped, each at the entrance to his tent. The LORD would speak to Moses face to face, as a man speaks with his friend. Then Moses would return to the camp. (Exodus 33:7-11)

If you've read this text before, or heard it taught, you know the usual takeaway is how Moses talked to God as a friend. This is a good and important lesson in regard to prayer and relationship, but I want to point out something more foundational. Namely, that Moses pitched a tent.

Something as simple as a "place" is crucial to your listening life. This has been understood from the beginning of Christian faith and history. Jesus would often go out into the hills, alone, to pray. As mentioned earlier, in the first through the third centuries, there was a group of men known as the Desert Fathers—though there were a few desert mothers thrown in there as well—who went out into the desert in order to pray and connect with God. The desert offered a place conducive to silence, and the opportunity to wait on God. It was seen as the place where one could experience revelation, conversion and transformation.

In his catalog of wisdom and sayings from the Desert Fathers of the fourth century, Thomas Merton tells of a certain brother who went to an abbot and asked him for a good word. The elder said to him, "Go, sit in your cell, and your cell will teach you everything." Listening to God usually involves going to a place that allows it. A place that provides a haven, the quiet, the space and opportunity to experience God. The idea of places of silence and solitude in order to hear God is terribly important. The Bible often describes the voice of God as something "still" or "small." A whisper, a prompting, a conviction. Yet our lives are filled with noise and stimulation, leaving little room for us to hear God in the deepest recesses of our spirit—and the conversation is, after all, Spirit to spirit.

So how does this conversation play out in life? It's simple; God will lead you. He will give his presence to you in ways that will guide you. Again, let's turn to the story of Moses:

> Moses said to the LORD, "You have been telling me, 'Lead these people,' but you have not let me know whom you will send with me. You have said, 'I know you by name and you have found favor with me.' If you are pleased with me, teach me your ways so I may know you and continue to find favor with you. Remember that this nation is your people."
>
> The LORD replied, "My Presence will go with you, and I will give you rest."
>
> Then Moses said to him, "If your Presence does not go with us, do not send us up from here. How will anyone know that you are pleased with me and with your people unless you go with us? What else will distinguish me and your people from all the other people on the face of the earth?"
>
> And the LORD said to Moses, "I will do the very thing you have asked, because I am pleased with you and I know you by name." (Exodus 33:12-17)

You know that the Christian faith is about a personal relationship with God through Christ. What may be lacking is the third member of the Trinity. Don't fall prey to a functional binitarianism that embraces two members of the Trinity and forgets about the third. To hear from God, to be led by God, is to keep in step with the Spirit.

This is key to how God speaks and leads. We want a detailed road map; he offers himself as a guide. We want a three-year strategic plan; he offers daily direction. Maddening though it can be, the Christian life is a Spirit-led life, and he leads as he chooses. The Bible speaks of it as the blowing of the wind, so expect both tornadic rushes and subtle breezes. The key is to be fluid as a weathervane, able to move instantly with any movement of air.

## THE LISTENING MATRIX

I wish for you one of the most important skill sets any follower of Christ can develop. It's a listening matrix. A simple but effective set of pursuits that you can take into your tent and with them cultivate a sensitive hearing for the voice of God. You know most of these pursuits, I'm sure, but perhaps haven't brought them together to hear a Word from God and experience his lead.

It begins with the Bible. If you want to know what God says to you about something, go to what he has already said about it. Which means the Bible. Because that's what the Bible is—God's word to you and your life. His *revelation*. The word *revelation* comes from the Latin word *revelatio*, which means to "draw back the curtain." Think of the stage of a theater. Only when the curtain is drawn back can we see what lies behind and, most of all, the story to be told. The authors of the Bible contend that their writings contain God revealing himself and truth about himself which could not otherwise be known. As such, the Bible really is God's Word reaching out toward us, informing us, and connecting with us about the deepest of truths.

Let me put this as simply as I know how: the Bible is God's Word to you and your life. He has spoken, definitively, and it's been captured for us in its pages. If you want to hear the voice of God, go to the archive of recordings he has made for you.

If that doesn't give you what you need—or you need some help discerning what the Bible is saying, go to people who walk with God who will share from the overflow of their life walking with

God and studying his word. This is the second part of the matrix: godly counsel.

Now let me tell you what I mean by "godly." These are people who walk with God, who have immersed themselves in his Scriptures, and have lived long enough to have that knowledge and experience come together and form a very rare commodity in our day: *wisdom*. Today we have information overload. We can surf the net and get anything we want. We are inundated with facts and figures, images and opinions. But what many don't have is wisdom. That is because wisdom takes time. It isn't something googled. Which is why we need mentors—people whom God can speak *through*. What these people have to say may not be a direct word from God, we all know that. But if you go to someone who is intimate with God, who has walked with God for many years, who has devoted himself or herself to the Scriptures, whose life is a testimony to the authenticity between those Scriptures and their life—someone who will not just tell you what you want to hear, but truly give you their best, most heartfelt, prayed-up counsel they have—then God can use them to speak to you.

In fact, the Bible encourages seeking godly counsel. Notice how strong a theme it is in the great wisdom book of the Bible, Proverbs, alone:

> The way of a fool seems right to him, but a wise man listens to advice. (Proverbs 12:15)

> He who walks with the wise grows wise. (Proverbs 13:20)

> Plans fail for lack of counsel, but with many advisers they succeed. (Proverbs 15:22)

> Listen to advice and accept instruction, and in the end you will be wise. (Proverbs 19:20)

> Make plans by seeking advice. (Proverbs 20:18)

So seek out some folks who can be this, and do this, for you. And I do mean *seek them out*. The tendency among many is to think that people like this don't exist. A cynicism builds inside them from the lack of integrity they've seen among fallen heroes, both political and spiritual. So they think everyone is a phony. Or at least that they're unavailable to offer advice. Many, if not most, come from broken homes where the wisdom that could have flowed from father or mother was broken and destroyed.

You know what I've found? We have a generation of young people desperate for mentors and counselors, and a generation of old folk eager to pour into the lives of the young. The young folk feel the older ones don't care, or don't have the time; the older folk feel the younger ones aren't interested in anything they might have to offer. So a young woman, desperate for an older woman to talk with about life and sex, marriage and relationship, child rearing and prayer, sits alone; and the older woman, rich with wisdom and maturity, insight and experience, sits alone. All when both would like to be sitting together.

The third part of the listening matrix has to do with prayer, which has been laced throughout this conversation. Here we *do* need to attend to the observation that Moses and God talked as two people face-to-face, as friends. It's easy to reduce prayer to talking *at* God, instead of talking *with* God. Most of us think of prayer as one-way communication. We have something to say, and we want God to listen, to hear, to respond. What we don't think about is prayer being a two-way conversation. But it is. Prayer is about conversation, communication and communion with the living God. It's entering into a dialogue with him.

How does that happen? As mentioned, usually quietly, through our spirits, in a still, small voice that is often like an impression or a sense. When we pray, we focus our thoughts on God, and when we do that, we get in tune with all that he is and all that he might want to say to us. Prayer might be considered the way we tune into his broadcast frequency. When I quiet myself, and begin to pray—and not just talk, but try to silently reflect on God and all that he is and has done, opening myself up to whatever he might want to say to me—I gain a clarity, an insight into life that comes in no other way. I gain crystal-clear impressions of God's leading, God's wisdom, God's direction. I get a perspective that is informed by God and his perspective. This is the idea behind the words to the song recorded in the forty-sixth psalm: "Be quiet and know that I am God" (Psalm 46:10 NCV 1991). The words *be quiet* mean to "let go," to "cease," to "stand still." Which means stopping long enough to focus in on God and hear what it is he might be saying. Or as another psalm puts it, "I pray . . . and wait for what he'll say and do" (Psalm 130:5 *The Message*).

## WHAT JESUS DID

This was precisely the way Jesus practiced his listening ear:

> Very early in the morning, while it was still dark, Jesus got up, left the house and went off to a solitary place, where he prayed. Simon and his companions went to look for him, and when they found him, they exclaimed: "Everyone is looking for you!" (Mark 1:35-37)

The first thing we notice about the life of Jesus is that he began the day with God. His life was marked by rising early enough to start his day oriented toward God. We'll talk more about this later. The second thing we notice was that his time with the Father was *quality* time, involving silence and solitude. This seemed to mark the life of Jesus, for in another section of the Bible, we read that "Jesus often slipped away to be alone so he could pray" (Luke 5:16 NCV). And once alone, surrounded by quiet, Jesus prayed, and evidently, would often study and reflect upon the Scriptures. This last component is something of an inference from his life, but a very compelling one. When Jesus was tempted by Satan, his response was always the same: "It is written . . . it is written . . . it is written" (Matthew 4:4, 7, 10). When he talked with people, one of his most frequent questions was, "Haven't you read this Scripture?" (Mark 12:10). When asked a question, he would often deal with it in the way described in this scene from Luke's Gospel: "Then Jesus quoted them passage after passage from the writings of the prophets, beginning with the book of Genesis and going right on through the Scriptures, explaining what the passages meant" (Luke 24:27 LB).

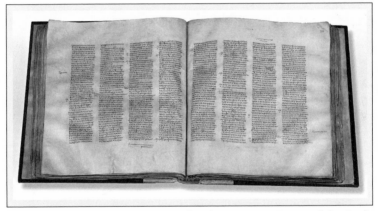

Figure 3.4: 5470. *Codex Sinaiticus* is a fourth-century manuscript of the Greek Bible, written between A.D. 330–350. Originally it contained the whole of both Testaments; today, only portions of the Greek Old Testament, or Septuagint, survive, along with a complete New Testament. It was discovered in 1844 by Constantine Tischendorf in St. Catherine's Monastery in Sinai, where parts of it are located today. Used by permission. Zev Radovan/BibleLandPictures.com

The impact of Jesus' time with the Father was profound. Take another look at our glimpse into his life, coupled with what immediately followed:

Very early in the morning, while it was still dark, Jesus got up, left the house and went off to a solitary place, where he prayed. Simon and his companions went to look for him, and when they found him, they exclaimed: "Everyone is looking for you!" Jesus replied, "Let us go somewhere else—to the nearby villages—so I can preach there also. That is why I have come." So he traveled throughout Galilee, preaching in their synagogues and driving out demons. (Mark 1:35-39)

Jesus was affected in three distinct ways as a result of this time. First, Jesus became *redirected.* He said, "Let us go somewhere else." He gained a clear, fresh understanding of the will of the Father for his life. It became clear what he was to do and where he was to go. Second, Jesus became *refueled,* saying ". . . so I can preach there also." He was ready for new tasks, new challenges. Before, it was as if his spiritual tanks were running low; after his time with God the Father, he was refueled and ready to continue on with his mission. Third, Jesus became *resolved,* committed to the big picture of his priorities and life purpose. With new clarity, he could say, "This is why I have come."

I've been in prayer and felt the need to call someone, write someone a note, give a financial gift, stop and help somebody on the side of the road, cancel a day's schedule and spend some time with my wife or kids, or do something radically differently than I had planned. And then, when I have followed through on those promptings from God through the Holy Spirit, it's amazing what I've experienced. Somebody will say, "You know, I'm really glad you called. You'll never know how much I needed that." Or I'll hear, "You know, that note you sent me came at just the right time." Even more exciting are those blazing insights you'll receive in regard to a decision, a course of action, or a way of life. I've walked away from prayer with a deep sense of the importance of saying yes, saying no, moving forward, slowing things up, changing direction.

Now, a word of caution here. This isn't meant to be wildly subjective—you pray, you feel something, you tell yourself it must be God's will, so you do it. God will never prompt you—even through prayer—to do anything that goes against his moral will. Promptings, and even feeling a peace about something, are subjective feelings, and can be very misleading. So if you think you're hearing a prompting to do something that goes against Scripture, you can rest assured that it wasn't an authentic prompting. But if it doesn't violate the moral will of God, and through prayer, you believe God is impressing something on you in relation to his will, pay attention. It's called a burning bush.

## Capturing What You Hear

Over the course of a lifetime, you'll want to record what God has said to you. A way of capturing this "listening" often involves journaling, a written record of thoughts and prayers to God, of God, and for God that flow from our quiet times. I confess that I have had a difficult relationship with journaling over the years, feeling almost repulsed by its recorded, almost public, nature. I was far too self-conscious to pour out my secret thoughts and feelings on paper for fear that it would be found and read. I also felt that if I did journal, I would be too tempted to write as if one day the journals would be found, perhaps even published posthumously, and thereby tempted to adopt a false and unrealistic tone to ensure my place in spiritual folklore. Yet I never could quite escape the *idea* of journaling, however much I may have chafed at the thought of the practice of the discipline. Too many Christians have found it to be of service—too many men and women I respected recommended its use.

So I began, but on my own terms. For many, journaling is the pouring out of every thought, every prayer, creating a running spiritual diary. For me, it is simply a place to capture what God seems to be trying to tell me, to do with me, to reveal to me—about myself, and himself. When such spiritual insights come, they are precious. In the past, I had scribbled them down on notes, kept them tucked away in a file, on my desk, or in a drawer, but they were soon lost or forgotten. I have come to realize that I simply cannot afford this. I need them grouped together, available for review, reflection, remembrance—and most importantly, continued application.

So I have journals, and they have taken years to fill. I tend to write in them only on monthly spiritual retreats. But I can now attest to the power they hold in terms of going back and reading previous entries. Quite simply, they help me remember what God has said to me, things I need to keep hearing.

## One Last Component

The listening matrix has one final component. It seems obvious, but it's actually quite easy to overlook. Make sure you are open to whatever God says. That you are ready to receive his word to your life, whether you like it or not. Otherwise, why bother? It's just a game. And God will speak to you. He will tell you things to start, things to stop. He'll prompt you to sacrifice, and even do things that might look foolish in the eyes of the world. He'll push the frontiers of faith, and challenge the most rooted of sins.

All to say, listening to God is not safe. But the good news is that this means neither is the person who listens. At least, safe to stay the *same*. They are too busy moving forward. They are, after all, being led.

# 4

## THE APARTHEID MUSEUM JOHANNESBURG, SOUTH AFRICA

### YOU ARE CALLED INTO COMMUNITY

*Not what a man is in himself as a Christian, his spirituality and piety, constitutes the basis of our community. What determines our brotherhood is what that man is by reason of Christ. Our community with one another consists solely in what Christ has done to both of us.*

DIETRICH BONHOEFFER, LIFE TOGETHER

Figure 4.1: Used by permission of the Apartheid Museum, South Africa/www.apartheidmuseum.org.

SOUTH AFRICA WAS RULED, since its independence from Britain in 1931 until its end in 1994, under a system that was later to become known as *apartheid*, meaning "apartness" in Afrikaans. It was a system designed to perpetuate the rule and privileges of the white minority on the grounds that black South Africans were not capable of self rule. Under apartheid, blacks could not travel on "whites only" buses, picnic on "whites only" beaches or take their sick children to "whites only" hospitals.

I can honestly say that I grew up fairly color blind. It began with the great love of my childhood, Catherine, a dear African American woman who cared for me as a boy. Catherine loved me like few others, and I her. On my birthday, she would hide candy bars in my bed to the number equaling my age; we would get inside sleeping bags and slide-race each other down the stairs; she would always make me my favorite lunch, macaroni and cheese. One day I came home from school and Catherine was waiting for me in our kitchen. Although trying to hide it from me, she had been crying. I remember feeling so upset—what had made my Catherine cry? I asked her what was wrong, and she simply said that a great man had died that day. I discovered later it was Martin Luther King Jr.

I didn't face racism until much later in life. I was born in Chicago, and then raised out West in Los Angeles and then later Seattle. Moving from Seattle to a small coastal town in North Carolina, just before my sophomore year in high school, was nothing less than a culture shock. I had always played basketball, and had played for my high school as a freshman in Seattle. I went out for the North Carolina team, and soon discovered that I was one of only two white boys who did. At that school, white boys played football, and black boys played basketball. I made the team, and loved those guys. But many of the whites called me "Oreo," after the cookie. Get it? A little bit of white in the middle of black.

But there was more community on those long bus rides back from games, listening to the Commodores and Parliament on my teammates' "boom boxes" than anything I had ever experienced before.

Now flash forward . . . I was in Johannesburg, South Africa, in 2004 on the very day when the tenth anniversary of the ending of apartheid was celebrated. During my time there, I went to the Apartheid Museum. There are two entrances. When you buy your ticket, you are randomly assigned to one or the other. You then find out that one is the "White" entrance, and the other is the "Non-White" entrance. You are only allowed entrance through the door of your race. It's then you realize that the entire museum experience places you under apartheid.

I was assigned to be black, and had to enter that way, and experience what that would be like. I felt everything you might imagine —awkward, ashamed, sick to my stomach that humans would ever treat each other that way. But most of all, I felt the evil of it all. Because it *was* evil. It was the antithesis of God's call on your life, and mine, which is to enter into community with others. A gathering of old and young, black and white, male and female, rich and poor. And most foundationally, to be able to join with others and experience life as *family* that is both holistic and healthy.

## LONGING FOR COMMUNITY

I know you long for authentic community. I do too. We have been born into an age of broken homes and the loss of our most precious and formative community, the family. And we both know what a poor substitute social media is for our longing to experience life with others. Indeed, that's why the Bible tells us that "God sets the lonely in families" (Psalm 68:6).

He did me.

My family of origin was not a particularly close one, and we

had, at best, a rocky existence. We moved frequently, so friendships were rare. Before I entered college, I had been in four elementary schools, two middle schools and three high schools.

I recall a night in elementary school. A new friend I'd made
through Little League baseball, Doug, invited me to spend the
night at his house. I eagerly accepted.

We ate together with his family. They actually sat down around
a table and ate. And they were civil, even loving toward each other.
There was a warmth that was palpable, and the laughter flowed
freely. Then Doug's dad went outside with us in the back yard. We
got our mitts and played catch. Then we loaded up the back of
their pickup truck with pillows and beanbag chairs and went to a
drive-in movie. No one argued on the way or sulked. They seemed
genuinely happy to be together. Doug's dad backed the truck up,
and we all got in the truck bed to watch the movie. It was one of
the most wonderful nights of my life. I walked away with a single
longing: one day, I want a family like that.

I think this generation is more focused on community than almost any other in recent memory because of the combined repug-
nancy of things like racism, and the breakup of the family structure that used to provide the foundation for community. Together,
we are both simultaneously passionate for it, and empty of it. The
longing we have is a good thing. It's also a God-thing.

## CREATED FOR COMMUNITY

Community is part of our very creation. The Christian doctrine of
the Trinity teaches that God is triune—three Persons, yet one
God—God the Father, God the Son and God the Holy Spirit. The
Trinity is a radical mystery, but the headline that is most important is the easiest to grasp: God himself exists in community. He
*is* community: perfect, complete, whole *community*. So when the
Bible tells us that this triune God created people in his image—an

image that, at its heart, is community—we are given an insight into our existence that must not be overlooked. We were created to be in community with *him* and with each *other.*

Brent Curtis and John Eldredge write of it this way:

> Think of your best moments of love or friendship or creative partnership, the best times with family or friends around the dinner table, your richest conversations, the acts of simple kindness that sometimes seem like the only things that make life worth living.
>
> Like the shimmer of sunlight on a lake, these are reflections of the love that flows among the Trinity. We long for intimacy because we are made in the image of perfect intimacy.

This is why the Bible talks about the creation of human beings in light of community. We read that after God created Adam, he said, "It is not good for the man to be alone. I will make a helper suitable for him" (Genesis 2:18). We were not made to live in isolation. We were made for community. Thus the longing of our hearts for community reflects the very nature of our design. So when we ache inside because we are lonely, when a single person longs for marriage, when a married person is torn apart

Figure 4.2: Guinnog/Wikimedia Commons

because of a dysfunctional relationship, when our stomachs turn over racism—there is a reason. Those things war against our being. The purpose of our creation—our very nature—is at hand.

But it's so screwed up. When you drive up to the Apartheid Museum, you are struck by the starkness of the building's form, which you are told was intentional, reminiscent of apartheid's spiritual impoverishment. You also discover that the harsh lines and raw brick walls are meant to bring to mind the poverty forced on so many through apartheid's laws and penalties. The wide use of steel and cement speak the universal language of oppression; fear and menace penetrate the dark images on walls and monitors. Color is noticeably absent everywhere, purposeful testimony to a time when hope was in small supply. The entire museum is a visual testimony to the fallen nature of human community.

We could spend much time on the effects of sin and the Fall on our relational lives. There is little doubt that much of our relational pain and longing will never be satisfied in this life. It is a broken world, and we are broken people. There is no perfect family, no perfect marriage, no perfect friend. All communities will disappoint because they are made up of sinful people like you and I. That doesn't mean community cannot be experienced; it can. Imperfect, yes, but still real and tangible. Love and grace break through into this darkened world in ways that shine into our lives. But not how you might think—or even want.

Here's why: community is not about you. Or me. If community becomes something we feel entitled to, something that must be provided for us, we have missed its great dynamic. Much talk about community today is very self-centered. We look for places and people to give it to us, even be it to us, and of course, keep it healthy for us. But real community isn't about an organization that provides you with friends, fulfills you relationally, or fixes all of your hurts. That would be confusing community with therapy.

The real goal of community is to so reflect the community of the Trinity that the watching world wants to join in.

Let me dig down a bit deeper. If you are not now, you may long to be married. And, if you're honest, it's for what it will bring to your life. Marriage isn't about what you will give, or even sacrifice, for your spouse; it is about the completion, the fulfillment, you feel you will gain. But that's not community, much less the foundation of marriage. Community is marked by selflessness; it is gauged by servanthood; and it is honored by the radical giving of grace. The heart of marriage is the longing to give of yourself, not to be given to.

## CONTACTING VERSUS CONNECTING

One of the great myths of relational life is that community is something *found*. In this fairy tale, community is simply out there—somewhere—waiting to be discovered like Prince Charming finding Cinderella. All you have to do is find the right person, join the right group, get the right job or become involved with the right church. It's kind of an "Over the Rainbow" thing; it's not here, so it must be "over" there.

Which is why so many people—and you've seen them, and probably flirted with it yourself—go from relationship to relationship, city to city, job to job, church to church, looking for the community that they think is just around the corner if they could only find the right people and the right place. The idea is that real community exists, *somewhere*, and we simply must tap into it. It's not something you have to work at; in fact, if you have to work at it, then you know it's not real community.

This mindset runs rampant in our day. If you have to work at community in a marriage, you must not be right for each other. If you have to work on community where you are employed, you've got a bad boss, or bad coworkers, or a bad structure. If you have to work at community in a neighborhood, you just picked the wrong subdivision. If you have to work on things with people in a church, well, there are obviously just problems with the church, or its leadership, or . . . yep, its "community."

I cannot stress enough how soundly unrealistic, much less un-biblical, this is. Community is not something you find; it is something you *build*. What you long for isn't about finding the right mate, the right job, the right neighborhood, the right church—it's about *making* your marriage, *making* your workplace, *making* your neighborhood and *making* your church the community God intended. Community is not something discovered; it is something *forged*. I don't mean to suggest any and all relationships are designed for, say, marriage. Or that there aren't dysfunctional communities you should flee from. My point is that all relationships of worth are products of *labor*.

This is why the Bible talks about people needing to form and *make* communities, not just come together as a community or "experience" community. It's why principles are given—at length—for how to work through conflict. It's why communication skills are articulated in the Bible, and issues such as anger are instructed to be dealt with. It's why the dynamics of successfully living with someone in the context of a marriage, or family, is explored in depth. As the author of Hebrews put it so plainly, "So don't sit around on your hands! No more dragging your feet . . . run for it! Work at getting along with each other" (Hebrews 12:12-14 *The Message*).

## Skills and Tools

But that raises a problem. You probably don't know how to work in such a way as to create community. Don't worry; you're not alone.

Benedictine oblate Kathleen Norris once wrote how several

monks told her that one of the biggest problems monasteries face is people who come to them "having no sense of what it means to live communally." They have been "schooled in individualism," and often had families that were so disjointed that even sitting down and having a meal together was a rarity. As a result, "they find it extremely difficult to adjust" to life in community.

Monks called into monastic life feeling unprepared for relational life? Welcome to our world. We spend years in school to prepare for a career without having to take a single class on getting along with a coworker. We spend months planning a wedding, meeting with caterers and photographers and wedding directors, and never once have to check off exploring what's involved in communicating with our spouse. We go through prenatal classes, decorate the nursery and set up the college fund, and never even think about how we're going to interact with them as a teenager. Add in our flaming depravity, and things really get sketchy. Running alongside our longing for community is a deep current of anticommunity behavior. We are filled with anger and envy, pride and competition. We do not naturally extend grace or forgiveness. We seldom take the high road, and we usually assume the worst of others.

Little wonder that the halls of the museum in Johannesburg feature displays of nooses and weapons—both sophisticated and homemade—as armed struggle took resistance to a new level. The museum does not attempt to hide that it was a nation in flames. Yet despite this chaos came the release of Nelson Mandela after twenty-seven years in prison, two years of peace negotiations, the building of bridges, and eventually, the birth of a democracy.

What is missing from most of our visions is a picture of community. It's like trying to put together a jigsaw puzzle without the picture on the box. One of our family traditions is putting together a jigsaw puzzle on New Year's Eve. We lay out the pieces on our kitchen table and invite anyone and everyone to put it together. Of course, the picture on the box is always front and center. Why?

Figure 4.3: NJR ZA/Wikimedia Commons

Without a sense of what we're trying to produce, we're just putting pieces together in random, haphazard ways, hoping something good comes out in the end.

So what is the picture on the community box? Between 1994 and 1996, South Africa's new democracy drew up a constitution marked by seven values that are commemorated by seven pillars standing in the courtyard entrance of the museum: democracy, equality, reconciliation, diversity, responsibility, respect and freedom. The Bible calls it "shalom."

## SHALOM

Shalom is commonly understood to mean "peace" or "health" or "prosperity." It carries within it the idea of "completeness." Cornelius Plantinga writes that the word *shalom* is "the webbing together of God, humans, and all creation in justice, fulfillment, and delight." Shalom is the vision of community; it is what community strives to be. With his characteristic blend of insight and humor, author John Ortberg netted out what that would mean:

In a world where shalom prevailed, all marriages would be healthy and all children would be safe. Those who have too much would give to those who have too little. Israeli and Palestinian children would play together on the West Bank; their parents would build homes for one another. In offices and corporate boardrooms, executives would secretly scheme to help their colleagues succeed; they would compliment them behind their backs. Tabloids would be filled with accounts of courage and moral beauty. Talk shows would feature mothers and daughters who love each other deeply, wives who give birth to their husband's children, and men who secretly enjoy dressing as men.

Disagreements would be settled with grace and civility. There would still be lawyers, perhaps, but they would have really useful jobs like delivering pizza, which would be nonfat and low in cholesterol. Doors would have no locks; cars would have no alarms. Schools would no longer need police presence or even hall monitors; students and teachers and janitors would honor and value one another's work. At recess, every kid would get picked for a team. . . .

No one would be lonely or afraid. People of different races would join hands; they would honor and be enriched by their difference and be united in their common humanity.

And in the center of the entire community would be its magnificent architect and most glorious resident: the God whose presence fills each person with unceasing splendor and ever-increasing delight.

Beautiful, isn't it? It reminds me of something I once read about Mother Teresa. When asked how she could give so much of herself to the poor, she would always say that when she looked at them, she saw Jesus in a distressing disguise. That is the heart of authentic community: being Jesus *to* others, and seeing Jesus *in* others. If we're married, we are interacting with our spouse as if unto him. If we're a child, we're obeying as if unto him. If an employee, we're working as if we're working for him. And the reverse is true: we're parenting as if we're parenting for him; we're leading others as if we're leading for him.

It's a radical idea. Even more radical is what such shalom is built on. Namely, grace. Grace, at its heart, is getting what you don't deserve, and not getting what you do. Grace is the essence of any successful relationship. Grace toward other people's differences. Grace applied toward other people's weaknesses. Grace applied toward other people's sins.

In his book *The One Thing*, Marcus Buckingham talks about some fascinating research on married couples. They studied these couples for twenty years, trying to find the common denominators among the couples that were happy, the ones that were highly compatible. Going in to the research, their theory was simple and understandable: the couples that were the happiest together were the ones who knew each other the best, and had consequently lowered their expectations over time so that they were rarely if ever disappointed with each other, which in turn let them stay together and stay in love. They expected that the happiest, most compatible couples were going to be the people who were so realistic in their estimation of each other that it facilitated their ability to stay together.

What they discovered in those happily married couples was the exact *opposite:* when one of the people in the relationship did something really ridiculous and created a break in their relationship, in the happily married couples, the other person in the relationship would automatically believe the best about them. They would come up with an explanation in their minds as to why she was late again, why he wasn't on time, why she spent so much money and why he had to travel so much. In their minds they fabricated a belief system and then chose to believe, over time, the best of their spouse. In other words, love really was blind.

People who are really in love, and stay in love, have such an inflated view of their spouse that even when their spouse totally screws up, they say, "Well, yeah, that did happen, but I'm sure there's a reason. I'm sure that as soon as he gets home and we talk about it it's going to work out."

I know what you're thinking . . . "Well, that's kind of living in denial." And in some respects it is. But if it results in a happy marriage, I'm all for denial, aren't you? I once heard a fellow pastor, Andy Stanley, talk about this, saying how important this is for relational health. Think about it: Do you really want to be married to someone who truthfully points out your flaws every single day?

"Honey, I see you are still overweight."

"Honey, your nose is still a bit crooked."

"You're still short."

They can point these things out every single day, and they would be absolutely right. They would be telling you the absolute truth. And you would be extraordinarily unhappy. Do you really want a friend who consistently points out all the things that are wrong with you? Or do you want close friends who overlook your faults and love you anyway—and just believe the best?

We know the answer.

So what did the research really discover in couples?

Grace.

And that is quite the challenge. Not that we don't like grace— we do. Not that we don't want to experience grace—we do. It's just that we are better at receiving it than giving it. But it is precisely the giving of grace that allows us to work through the relational stages that afford community.

You know the stages. You've lived with them your whole life.

The first stage is usually some kind of general *attraction*. Not many people instantly hit you wrong. Usually there is something there that's likable, or at least you're openly neutral. So stage one is extending a general welcome to the relationship.

But you know what that stage is almost always followed by? *Disappointment*. You start off by viewing someone from a relational distance. All you have are short, quick interactions that haven't been subjected to the test of time. But once you get to know someone *beyond* that level, you start to see their dark side. And they *will have* a dark side. They *will have* weaknesses. Differences. Sins. Now here's our tendency—to let the second stage of disappointment be the defining stage in your relationship with someone. Sometimes it's called for. When you find out that someone's dark side is too strong to deal with, or you realize you've got an unsafe person on your hands, or that what you thought was chemistry turns out to be an allergy, then it's okay to let this stage be a wake-up call.

But a lot of the time, the differences that we often let end the relationship are trivial and we just don't extend the grace or maturity to let the relationship go through the necessary—yes, inevitable—disappointment stage. But if you don't work through it, you will never move on to the third stage, which is where real community begins to take place.

And that third stage is *acceptance*. This is when you work through the disappointments, you do the labor of extending grace and understanding, and from that allow yourself to come to a healthy understanding of someone's strengths and weaknesses. Then you accept them on those terms. The Bible specifically challenges us on this. In the book of Romans, it says: "Accept one another, then, just as Christ accepted you" (Romans 15:7). If you're not able to do this, you will *never* have meaningful relationships in your life. Ever.

If you are unable or unwilling to move into the stage of acceptance, then you will be a very lonely and isolated person. No human on earth is free of things that might disappoint you. If you don't believe this, you'll just go from person to person, relationship to relationship, and never have any of them move into real community. But if you'll journey through the second stage and into the third, then you can move into the fourth stage—which is *appreciation*. This is getting back to what you found attractive about the person to begin with, and enjoying all that is good and wonderful about them. It's almost like a return to the first stage, but with wisdom and insight. If the first stage is like a first date, the fourth stage is like a fiftieth wedding anniversary, seeing the look in one another's eyes—the deep, mature sense of love you share. And it's a beautiful thing.

Is there anything more? Yes. *Intimacy:* a fifth stage where you can love and be loved, serve and be served, celebrate and be celebrated, and know and be known.

So do you see how the work of commitment is key? Too many of us have a brightly illuminated "Exit" sign over every relationship in our life—where we work, where we live, where we go to church, even in our marriages. As long as we hang that sign over the door of our community life, we won't do the work of commitment that is needed to *experience* the community we *long* for. The secret of the best friendships, the best marriages, the best job situations and churches and neighborhoods, is that they've taken down the exit signs. And when there is no exit sign, you have one and only one choice: do whatever it takes for the relationship to flourish.

I recently read of a family who brought home a twelve-year-old boy named Roger whose parents had died of a drug overdose. There was no one to care for him, so the parents of this family decided they would raise him as if he were one of their own sons. At first, it was difficult for Roger. This was the first environment he had ever lived in that was free of heroin-addicted adults. As a result of the culture shock, every day—and several times during the day—either Roger's new mom or dad would say, "No, Roger, that's not how we behave in this family." Or "No, Roger, you don't have to scream or fight or hurt other people to get what you want." Or "Roger, we expect you to show respect in this family." In time, Roger began to change.

For so many of us, community—particularly the new community that the Bible calls us to—demands new behavior. The death of old practices, and the birth of new ones. We're like the boy, adopted into a new family, needing to relearn how to interact with people.

But here's the good news: When we hear the Holy Spirit say to us, "No, that's not how we act in this family," we can say, "You're right. It's not." And change. And begin to have the relationships with others we want as part of the new community God desires for us to experience.

## When Community Breaks Down

But what do you do when community breaks down? How do you resolve conflict with someone in a constructive, positive way? The turning point in South African history took place in the late 1980s. In 1988, while still in prison, Nelson Mandela extended an invitation to the government to negotiate an end to apartheid. Fast-forward in time, and you have the election of 1994—seen by many as a miracle—and one of the only times in history that a colonizing group gave up its power without a civil war or large-scale external intervention.

But how are such negotiations made? Not just between rival factions in a country torn apart by the sin of racism, but between men and women, husbands and wives, daughters and sons? These reconciliations are essential for community in your life. And the Bible points us down a clear, simple and direct path. It has eight steps.

*Step 1: Go directly.* The first step is to go directly to the person with whom you are having the conflict. Here's what Jesus said about this: "If you are offering your gift at the altar and there remember that your brother has something against you, leave your gift there in front of the altar. First go and be reconciled to your brother; then come and offer your gift" (Matthew 5:23-24). And not only are we to go, but to go quickly. In Ephesians, the Bible says: "Do not let the sun go down while you are still angry" (Ephesians 4:26). The Bible teaches unequivocally that the healthiest way to resolve a problem with another person is to go immediately and directly to that person. This is sitting across from someone and saying, "Listen, I've sensed some tension between us, and I'd like to talk about it with you. If I've offended you, I want to own it and ask for your forgiveness. But no matter what the issue is, I'd like for us to try and work through it."

*Step 2: Go privately.* The second step is that when you go, go privately. Jesus taught this in Matthew 18:15: "If your brother sins against you, go and show him his fault, just between the two of you" (Matthew 18:15). The temptation will be to go to six of our friends, tell them our problem, and paint the person as a jerk and us as the victim. Or as John Ortberg once wrote, his tendency is to go to someone else and say, "Let me tell you what's going on here. I just want to lay it out objectively and get some feedback from a neutral third party. Don't you share my concerns about this person, who is my brother in Christ and a deeply disturbed psychopath?" When you do that, you'll feel better for a little while because you've got it off your chest, but all you would have done is practice and then cement your anger, or resentment, or sense of offense and hurt.

*Step 3: Begin with affirmation.* Once you go to the person and sit down privately with them, the third step the Bible gives is strategic: start off with affirmation. In Ephesians 4, the Bible says, "Do not use harmful words when talking. Use only helpful words, the kind that build up and provide what is needed, so that what you say will do good to those who hear you" (Ephesians 4:29 GN). If you're like me, when you talk to somebody about an area of conflict, your first tendency won't be to affirm—it will be to accuse. It won't work, and it won't help. If you go in with the mindset that you are simply the victim—completely closed to the idea that you might be a bit at fault as well—you aren't going to be able to resolve much of anything. Scott Peck, in his book on community building, says that when it comes to conflict resolution, we need to bring an "emptiness" to the table. In other words, we need to empty ourselves of whatever it is that might keep us from really listening to the other person. This means the prejudices that make us think that our view is the only view, that our feelings are the only feelings, that our memory is the only way to remember something that happened or our way of interpreting it is the only way to interpret it.

*Step 4: Monitor your mouth.* Step number four is to monitor your mouth. In Proverbs 15, the Bible says, "A gentle answer turns away wrath, but a harsh word stirs up anger" (Proverbs 15:1). This is different than number three—this isn't about beginning with affirmation; that's a step about what you say. This is a step about how you say it. Have you ever talked to someone, and the tone of their voice betrays everything they're saying? But a gentle answer, a gentle reply, a tone of voice that is consciously careful, can diffuse the entire situation. One of the best ways to do that is to express yourself with "I feel" statements. Just say, "I feel that there has been competition between us." Or "I feel that you don't care about what I'm going through." Or "I feel that sometimes I'm not as important to you as your job."

*Step 5: Look for what you can own.* The fifth step is to look—and look hard—for what you can own. In 1 John 1:8, the Bible says, "If we claim to be without sin, we deceive ourselves and the truth is not in us" (1 John 1:8). Now, most of us would be willing to own that in general, but this is about owning it specifically—in your relational life—particularly in relation to those you are in conflict with. Our tendency is to look for what accusations we can make that will stick. Almost like we're presenting a case to the jury. We come to blame, not to own. We come to accuse, not to admit. We come to point the finger, not accept the blame. Which isn't conflict resolution; it's confrontational assault. If we're going to resolve conflict, we have to be open to what we did wrong, what we misinterpreted, what we misunderstood, what we didn't know, mistakes we might have made, ways we could have reacted more positively, places where we could have given the benefit of the doubt, and times we didn't believe the best but assumed the worst.

*Step 6: Establish specific ways to resolve the conflict.* The sixth step is to establish some specific ways to resolve the conflict. The Bible lays this out in the book of Hebrews: "Work at getting along with each other" (Hebrews 12:14 *The Message*). And the key word there is *work*. You have to lay out some specific ways you are going to address the problem. There needs to be some kind of game plan, some kind of intentional effort you will make, flowing from your sit-down time with that person. For example, here are two great questions to put on the table: "How can we avoid this particular problem in the future?" And, "How can we improve our lines of communication?"

*Step 7: Reaffirm the relationship.* The seventh step is to reaffirm the relationship. What often happens is that we resolve the conflict, but then never consider going on to live in community with that person. We bite the bullet and take some of these steps to get the problem out on the table, but we go about it as if our goal is to walk away with a clear conscience so that we can unfriend the person on Facebook and feel good about it. But it's not about unfriending; it's about befriending. Which is why the Bible, in its great chapter on community in 1 Corinthians 13, says "Love . . . keeps no record of wrong" (1 Corinthians 13:5).

*Step 8: If needed, draw up boundaries.* Now for most situations, those seven steps are all that you need. You may need to camp out on one or more of the steps, or bring in others to aid the process if you hit a wall, and it may take some time to work through all of this. It may involve more than a single sitting at Starbucks, but the process itself works. God intended it to. It's his prescription for relational health. But occasionally there is an eighth step you may need to take. The eighth step, if needed, is to draw up some relational boundaries. This is when you've done all you can to resolve the conflict, or you are trying to, but you aren't being allowed to resolve it by the other person. That possibility has to be acknowledged.

Sometimes the other person is unwilling to engage in the process with you: they won't meet with you to go through this, much less empty themselves for the process, but the conflict rages. Sometimes they can even go on the warpath, making your life a living hell. You try to talk, but they won't meet with you; you try to help them understand, but they refuse to consider any other view but their own; you want to reconcile, but they choose to remain offended, or if they have been the aggressor, they insist on continuing to be an adversary. When that happens, the Bible has clear counsel: "Warn a quarrelsome person once or twice, but then be done with him. It's obvious that such a person is out of line, rebellious against God. By persisting in divisiveness he cuts himself off" (Titus 3:10-11 *The Message*).

If you want a contemporary word for the Bible's counsel, I would use the word *boundaries*. There comes a time when you have to relationally remove yourself from someone because they will not allow you to be in community with them. This is rare, and drastic, but sometimes you have no choice. But notice that this is the final step—not the first. It only comes after every possible investment has been made. Because the goal is never separation, but reconciliation.

## Memo from Robben Island

In many ways, this reconciliation process is my lasting thought from the Apartheid Museum—not the museum itself, but how for eighteen years, on the shores of Robben Island, Cell Block B housed a black man by the name of Nelson Mandela who, while in prison, became a Christian after watching a Billy Graham crusade on television. Released in 1994, he became the state president of South Africa. What led to such a turn of events? The former Anglican archbishop of Cape Town, Desmond Tutu, simply said, "Had Nelson Mandela . . . not been willing to forgive, we would not have even reached first base."

Figure 4.4: Paul Mannix/Wikimedia Commons

We think of the dream of community birthed in Mandela's heart, but too often forget Tutu's insight. It was not a community that happened naturally; it was forged through specific acts and decisions, mostly of the spirit. Or, as Mandela himself once wrote, "a refusal to hate." Which means an embrace of what it takes to love.

# 5

## CHARTRES CATHEDRAL
## CHARTRES, FRANCE

### YOU ARE SEXUAL

*Once upon a time the world was full of miracles.*
*And Chartres was of all places, one of the most miraculous.*

COLIN WARD

✦ ✦ ✦

Figure 5.1: Guillaume Piolle/Wikimedia
Commons

IF YOU EVER GET A CHANCE TO VISIT Paris, you will be tempted to spend every minute walking alongside its canals, getting lost in the Louvre, or exploring the back alleys of its many quarters (I'm personally fond of the Cour du Commerce St-Andre in St-Germain). If you take a day trip away from the famed city, you will undoubtedly be lured to nearby Versailles to see the opulent decadence of Louis XIV. Fair enough. But when you go, leave early enough to reboard the train after lunch for another stop or two, including the little village of Chartres (pronounced shar-tras) just forty miles or so southwest of Paris. If you do, you will experience one of the most holy places I have ever entered, and the site of millions of pilgrims who share my feelings.

The site of the church has been considered hallowed ground for many centuries, akin to such sites as Stonehenge, though we don't know why. You can take tours into its crypt and discover the ancient druid site the church rests over, along with a well that dates back to those times. There is some evidence that a church existed there as early as the fourth century. A fire in 1020 destroyed the building; it was rebuilt, only to be enveloped by fire again in 1194. When it was rebuilt from those ashes, what is arguably the world's most beautiful, and perhaps most sacred, cathedral was built.

Chartres is an ancient medieval cathedral that still retains the *sense* of being an ancient medieval cathedral. In fact, it is almost perfectly preserved in regard to the original design and details of its construction, which began in 1194. The current building set the standard for what came to be known as Gothic cathedrals, with a spire rising over three hundred feet and a nave that is over one hundred feet high.

Yet if you have heard of it at all, it would probably be because of its stained glass, considered to be the most beautiful of its kind that has ever been created. Chartres actually holds over eight thousand images in various mediums—a "pictorial encyclopedia encased in a stone binding" portraying "the whole drama of the Redemption, from the Creation to the Last Judgment." Today we are used to sight and sound extravaganzas; as Colin Ward notes, "We can only imagine how much more miraculous the windows of Chartres must have been for the pilgrims of the Middle Ages, accustomed to daylight, candlelight or rush-light, when they first encountered this incredible light show." The dazzling mixture of blue and ruby "seem to fulfill an active part in cathedral ritual—an incense of color."

When you first enter Chartres, you will want to look up and around at the famed stained glass. The rose window above the main portal dates from the thirteenth century, and the three windows beneath it contain what are arguably the finest examples of twelfth-century stained-glass artistry in the world. The oldest window, and I think the most beautiful, is the Notre-Dame de la Belle Verriere (Our Lady of the Lovely Window), in the south choir.

Figure 5.2: Wikimedia Commons

But don't forget to look down. There you will see an ancient prayer labyrinth on the floor. Historians assume it was placed there as a final penance for pilgrims who, it is believed, had to traverse its length on their knees. There was once a copper plaque in the center of the maze, now lost to time. Based on a description of its contents by an eighteenth-century scholar, the labyrinth portrayed man's path to God, not after death, but now, while here on earth.

I went there to see the famed windows, but this experience is what I have returned for time and again. I find entering any of the medieval cathedrals of Europe a moving experience, but none are more affecting than Chartres. Stone floors, vaulted ceiling, darkened interior . . . it transports you back in time, and calls you to a sense of reverence and reflection. "To enter Chartres is to enter an ethereal, glowing ambience." Chartres offers a fresh and enduring encounter with the sacred—not simply as a foretaste of the life to come, but as a challenge to the life at hand.

We need a sense of the sacred in our day, and from it, the holy. Even more, we need the sanctified lives it reminds us to live. When people spend time with us as Christians they should sense something about us that is not of this world, a life that holds something they do not possess. Sadly, there are few such encounters. Yet when I am in Chartres, I encounter that otherness in ways that overwhelm my senses.

And it affects me. I am driven to pray. I want to reflect, to go deep. I don't want to leave, for there I find myself longing to be the person I seldom am. It makes me want to lead a more holy life, because I am face-to-face with such a clear sense of the holy. Which is why I want to talk about sex; it is the holiest of cathedrals, and the most sacred of places, and where others should encounter us at our most different. And it is perhaps the one place where we are losing the distinctive nature of the life we are called to live more than any other.

Now, for some assumptions. I'm going to assume that you have a powerful sex drive and that you want to handle your sexual energies appropriately—and that you have found that this is not easy. In other words, you have found that what Jesus once said to Peter is true when he said, "The spirit is willing, but the body is weak" (Matthew 26:41). I am also going to assume you want to protect yourself against mismanaged sex urges, the kind that lead to pornography, premarital sex and adulterous affairs. And I am going to assume that you already face a lot of challenges trying to do just that.

With that in mind, let's begin with the truth about sex and its place in the cathedral of your body.

## Sex Is a God-Thing

The first truth about sex is that it is a God-thing. When people begin to study what the Bible has to say about sex, the first and most shocking truth they discover is that the Bible thinks sex is wonderful and beautiful because it is created and given by God. The Bible teaches that sex was part of God's desire and design for our bodies and lives. Here's the initial taste of what the Bible says about sex in the book of Genesis: "The LORD God said, 'It is not good for the man to be alone. I will make a helper suitable for him' . . . the LORD God made a woman . . . and he brought her to the man. For this reason a man will leave his father and mother and be united to his wife, and they will become one flesh. The man and his wife were both naked, and they felt no shame" (Genesis 2:18, 22, 24-25). In these opening verses of the Bible we have the clearest statement imaginable that God made Adam—a man—to want, need and desire a woman—Eve. And not just emotionally, but physically. They were to become one flesh. So sex is God's idea, God's design and God's creation.

Author Philip Yancey reflects on this in a way that drives home just how much attention God gave to this part of our life: "Having studied some anatomy, I marvel at God laboring over the physiology of sex: the soft parts, the moist parts, the millions of nerve cells sensitive to pressure and pain yet also capable of producing pleasure, the intricacies of erectile tissue, the economical and ironical combination of organs for excretion and reproduction, the blending of visual appeal and mechanical design. As the zoologists remind us, in comparison with every other species the human is bountifully endowed."

But that's not all the Bible points us to. Think again about that last line of that passage in Genesis. They were both naked, and felt *no shame*. That wasn't just because of a good weigh-in that week or some extra workouts at the gym. Under God's design, sex is something virtuous. It's not something dirty or cheap, sordid or immoral. It was meant to be openly embraced and unashamedly enjoyed.

Nowhere is this more clearly exhibited than in one of the most overlooked books in the Bible, the Song of Songs, where you find a beautiful, even erotic love poem between a man and his wife:

Kiss me—full on the mouth! Yes! For your love is better than wine, headier than your aromatic oils. (Song of Songs 1:2-3 *The Message*)

When my King-Lover lay down beside me, my fragrance filled the room. His head resting between my breasts—the head of my lover was a sachet of sweet myrrh. (Song of Songs 1:13 *The Message*)

How beautiful you are, my beloved, how beautiful! Your eyes are soft like doves. What a lovely, pleasant sight you are, my love, as we lie here on the grass. (Song of Songs 1:15-16 NLT)

Or my favorite,

> How beautiful you are, my darling! Oh, how beautiful! Your
> eyes behind your veil are doves. Your hair is like a flock of
> goats descending from Mount Gilead. Your teeth are like a
> flock of sheep just shorn, coming up from the washing. (Song
> of Songs 4:1-2)

That'll work.

But sex is more than good. It is more than pleasurable. It is
deeply, deeply holy and should be treated as such. When you enter
the great cathedrals of Europe, such as Chartres, there is an instant sense of standing on ground that is sacred. You naturally
speak in hushed tones, reflect on God's "otherness" and marvel at
the wonder of raw beauty. The power of the stone, glass, soaring
ceiling and candlelight does something to you. It opens your soul
in ways few other places—and experiences—can.

When Chartres was being built, the people "asked themselves
whether a building can lift the soul toward God by its structure
and its ornament." History's answer has been yes.

Sex is this way. The Bible tells us that God designed sex to do
something to the people who engaged in it. Experiencing that
which is sacred always does. In this case, it does something sacred
to both of you. Or, if misused, something spiritually damaging. As
the apostle Paul wrote, "There is more to sex than mere skin on
skin. Sex is as much spiritual mystery as physical fact . . . the two
become one" (1 Corinthians 6:16 *The Message*). Sex is sacred because of its power for relational intimacy. It is the mystical bonding of two people—a bonding that is unlike any other. As such, it
is to be reserved for the one we commit to in marriage.

But this is precisely what we have been conditioned to reject.

## The Lies We Believe

I recall an episode of the hit sitcom *Friends* where Monica asks one guy, "So, we can [just be] friends and have sex?" "Sure," he answers. "It'll just be something we do together, like racquetball."

In our current cultural context, nearly three-fourths of all high-school students say that they have had sex by the time they graduate. One out of every five listed at least half a dozen partners, and one out of every six said they'd lost their virginity by the age of thirteen. Health records indicate that the United States has the highest rate of teen pregnancy, teen abortion and teen childbirth in the industrialized world. According to the most comprehensive national survey of sexual behaviors released by the federal government, slightly more than half of all American teenagers, ages fifteen to nineteen, have engaged in oral sex, with males and females reporting similar levels of experience. A professor of pediatrics at the University of California–San Francisco observes that "at 50 percent, we're talking about a major social norm. It's a part of kids' lives." The report, released by the National Center for Health Statistics in Hyattsville, Maryland, shows that the figure increases to about 70 percent of eighteen- to nineteen-year-olds.

And it's not just among the young. For the first time in American history, households featuring married couples are in the minority. Married couples represented just 48 percent of American households in 2010, according to the 2010 Census. Compare this to 78 percent of households occupied by married couples in 1950.

And then there is the staggering number of people who pursue infidelity after marriage. Elliot Spitzer was a rising political star, first as New York State attorney general, then as governor—such a rising star that he was among the top names rumored to make a run for president. He was widely noted for probing Wall Street crimes, not to mention other moral issues, such as forcing music publishers to pay millions in back royalties to artists, punishing corporations involved in aiding acid rain, and participating in under-the-table commissions in the insurance industry. In 2002 he was named "Crusader of the Year." In 2003 he was named "Businessperson of the Year." In 2004 the University of Illinois awarded him with the "Ethics in Government" award. He had a beautiful wife and three teenage daughters. But as you probably know, he was forced to resign due to his involvement with a prostitution ring. It's now even being called the "Spitzer Syndrome." And he's not alone. It's affected everyone from presidents to pastors, CEOs to coaches, priests to professors.

Sex really is like fire. It is pure and purifying; it is also destructive. In the proper place and setting it is beautiful. If it operates outside of your fireplace, if it gets outside of where it belongs and where it is meant to be contained and harnessed and channeled, it can burn your house down and destroy everything you have.

This is part of a much larger cultural turn, of course. In the book *A Return to Modesty*, Wendy Shalit observed that we have lost our respect for one of the great classical virtues—that of sexual modesty. In her book *Real Sex*, author Lauren Winner begins by saying, "I write for those of us who have no memory of chastity."

Consider the evolution of a word which originated in the Middle Ages and is now commonplace in popular culture, marketing and casual conversation. *Slut.* One writer defined the term this way: "She is the one who will go home with you, the sure bet, the kind of girl you can lie down with and then walk all over." Such a word used to be a term of derision. It was a word you used to put someone down, to insult them. No girl wanted to be a slut. Now novelty shops and websites sell Slut lip balm, bubble bath, soap and lotion. A cocktail is known as the Red-Headed Slut. The word *slut* is used affectionately, positively, with teenagers even incorporating it into their instant-messaging screen names. Today teenagers will say, "Hi, slut!" the way earlier generations would say, "Hi, chick!" The editor-in-chief of *Seventeen* magazine noted that "today, 'slut,' even 'ho' . . . is used in a fun way, a positive way."

Cultivating an exhibitionistic, slutty appearance—donning the trappings of promiscuity—has been a growing influence on fashion and popular culture. Women wear T-shirts with provocative slogans. Stripping and pole dancing is the latest way to exercise and lose weight. And celebrities become celebrities for Internet sex videos.

But while such a word may have originated during the time of Chartres construction, it holds its place in our modern zeitgeist because we no longer have such symbols to remind us how base we have become. This is why holding to the sacred nature of the temple of your body is so essential. The Christian view of sexual fulfillment offers intimacy with another person, and with God, of such gravitas and weight and depth and meaning that it could not imagine any relationship less than marriage for it to be realized. Ironically, it is the promise of intimacy—not simply pleasure—that makes sexual activity so appealing. G. K. Chesterton once wrote something I've always found provocative. He said that everyone who walks into a brothel is actually looking for God. It's true. They are. Sex is one of the closest "God experiences" human life has to offer.

The tragedy is that sex outside of God's intended design, which is marriage, and outside of an understanding of its true nature, trivializes and then destroys the emotional union it was intended to provide as a complement to the lifelong commitment of marriage. No other human activity has the same power as sexual intimacy. It is the supreme expression of a relationship. It is ultimate emotional unity. That's why the Bible says in 1 Corinthians that "we must not pursue the kind of sex that avoids commitment and intimacy, leaving us more lonely than ever—the kind of sex that can never 'become one'" (1 Corinthians 6:17-18 *The Message*). Only within marriage can that level of emotional union, that level of relational bonding, take place without being violated or cheapened. When sex is divorced from that—when it becomes recreational, separate from commitment, it stops being wonderful. Which is why the Bible says, "Honor marriage, and guard the sacredness of sexual intimacy between wife and husband. God draws a firm line against casual and illicit sex" (Hebrews 13:4 *The Message*).

And we intuitively know it. It's why we cling to the vestiges of its sacred nature, even when we have abandoned its pursuit. This came home to me in an article I recently read about an account of a wedding. The bride wore a white gown, and a veil demurely covered her face. The groom slipped a ring on the bride's finger. After a lavish reception, the newlyweds flew off on their honeymoon. Yet the person attending the wedding found it all shallow and without meaning. For example, the white wedding gown symbolizes the purity of the bride. And yet all in attendance knew that the bride and groom had lived together for three years.

The ceremony took place in a church, even though the two were agnostics.

When the minister invited the groom to kiss the bride, everybody laughed. They all knew he'd already slept with her, so it seemed silly for someone to be giving him permission to kiss her.

The couple promised to stay married "till death do us part," but just in case, they had signed a binding pre-nuptial agreement.

As for the honeymoon—the traditional start of a couple's sex life—it was a case of "been there, done that."

Now, given that the average wedding costs around $30,000, why do people bother with all this? Why don't people go to the courthouse and skip the rituals which are so obviously empty? It's because we're not being honest with ourselves. We long for what God offers through sex, even though we have rejected it for our lives. When it comes time to marry, we search for the sacred, grasp for significance, and end up having to use the very symbols and rituals whose meanings we have rejected.

But there is much more at stake than the cheapening, or even undermining, of our relational world. If sex is hallowed ground, given by God, then its misuse and abuse will affect us spiritually. Every sex act involves the Holy Spirit—either reflecting his joy, or grieving his heart. The proper use of sex floods our souls with the Spirit's presence; the improper use drives him away.

Sin in any form is a direct offense against God that separates us from his love. That includes sexual sin. God created us. We are spiritual beings. Part of our creation was sexuality. When we misuse our bodies through sexual behavior, it tears away at our soul and drives God away. According to the apostle Paul, maybe more than any other sin: "There is a sense in which sexual sins are different from all others. In sexual sins we violate the sacredness of our own bodies, these bodies that were made for God-given and God-modeled love, for 'becoming one' with another. Or didn't you realize that your body is a sacred place, the place of the Holy Spirit?" (1 Corinthians 6:18-19 *The Message*).

I'm not sure why Paul felt sexual sin was so damaging to our relationship with God, but I have an idea. Sex was given to us for ultimate union and intimacy with the one we have committed our lives to. It reflects the intimacy within the Trinity, as well as the overflow of that love toward us. Indeed, the Hebrew word for "love" is *aheb*, and it was an earthy, almost lustful word, perhaps best translated as "panting after." This led the rabbis to substitute the word *hesed*, which translates into the tamer "lovingkindness." But God's love for us *is* full of desire. When we violate the nature of sexual intimacy, it is as if we are destroying the dynamic of spiritual intimacy with God as well. Our sexual fidelity so mirrors the nature of spiritual fidelity that to violate one is to violate the other.

## SEX, LIES AND CONVENTS

Few stories mirror the dangerous pull of sex, and the spiritual confusion it can cause, than that of Abelard and Heloise. In the same century Chartres burned and was subsequently rebuilt, Peter Abelard, a widely celebrated and influential philosopher and theologian, seduced, impregnated, agreed to marry, then forced into a convent a young woman by the name of Heloise.

It was a tabloid sex scandal designed for today's twenty-four-hour news cycle. He was a brilliant young intellectual who, by the age of twenty-one, was already the founder of his own school. With his fame came controversy, not least of which was through his book *Sic et Non* ("Yes and No"), a work that used questions born of skepticism to explore matters of faith and reason. She was more than twenty years his junior, an innocent teenage student, the niece of Canon Fulbert of Notre Dame.

Abelard set out to seduce the young woman, writing in his autobiography, "I . . . decided she was the one to bring to my bed, confident that I should have an easy success." After making arrangements to move into her home and serve as her tutor, he proceeded to take advantage of his position. By his own admission, there was "more kissing than teaching." It didn't stop with kissing, with Abelard adding: "Our desires left no stage of love making untried."

Her uncle soon stumbles upon the relationship, but not before Heloise realizes she is pregnant. "I protested that I had done nothing unusual in the eyes of anyone who had known the power of love," Abelard wrote, "and recalled how since the beginning of the human race women had brought the noblest men to ruin." Not surprisingly, this did little to appease the father. "To conciliate him further, I offered him satisfaction in the form he could never have hoped for: I would marry the girl I had wronged. All I stipulated was that the marriage should be kept secret so as not to damage my reputation."

Fulbert agreed, but anger ran deep. Heloise was sent to live with Abelard's family until she gave birth to a son, at which point Abelard placed her in a convent near Paris. The convent didn't help with the family's ongoing anger. "At this news her uncle and his friends and relatives imagined that I had tricked them, and had found an easy way of ridding myself of Heloise by making her a nun. Wild with indignation they plotted against me, and one night as I slept peacefully in an inner room in my lodging, they bribed one of my servants to admit them and there took cruel vengeance on me of such appalling barbarity as to shock the whole world; they cut off the parts of my body whereby I had committed the wrong of which they complained."

The castration brought Abelard to his spiritual senses, interpreting the attack as a blessing in disguise, freeing him from further sexual temptations. Free to serve God without lust, he entered a monastery and devoted himself to life in the cloisters.

Heloise blamed herself for all that had taken place. She was in love with Abelard. Initially refusing to marry him for fear of what it would do to his reputation, she offered herself as his lifelong mistress. She had no desire to be a nun, but would do anything to please her lover. But Abelard had moved on, coming to terms with his role as a monk to such a degree that he spent much of the rest of his life trying to convince Heloise to follow suit. He bought land and helped establish a new convent with Heloise as its abbess. He even helped develop the rule by which they would live as a community.

Things didn't go well with Abelard professionally. In 1141 his writings were condemned at the Council of Sens. He died before he could appeal the ruling to the pope. Heloise arranged for his burial in a plot at her convent where she could tend to his grave. She lived two more decades and became one of the great abbesses of medieval monasticism and her convent one of the most famous in France.

It was a strange irony that Abelard died a condemned man, but with a heart right with God; Heloise was celebrated for her faithful ministry, but as Ruth Tucker writes, "Whether Heloise ever came to terms with her tormented love and fully submitted to God will never be known."

## MORE DANGERS

There are, of course, other dangers related to violating God's design that are important to note. First, since sex was designed by God to foster intimacy and to make the two one, it needs the safety and boundaries of marriage to protect it from wounding us deeply. Apart from the commitment that comes with marriage, sex can be more violation than union.

I read of a man who was involved in numerous affairs, and he wrote that he felt like he had "left little bits of myself all over the place." You cannot walk away from sex unchanged. By its very definition, sex is the giving away of the essence of who you are to another person. It isn't just a one-night stand. It isn't something that has no significance. It isn't just a physical act. You've entered into oneness, and the separation of the one back into two always leaves damage to the soul. In the movie *Vanilla Sky*, Tom Cruise plays a man-about-town who ends a fling with a beautiful blonde he was never serious about. But she can't handle the breakup, so she pursues him to the point of stalking. When she finally corners him, she says: "Don't you know that when you sleep with someone, your body makes a promise whether you do or not?"

On an even more foundational level, recent research by sociologists has found a significant correlation between sexual restraint and emotional well-being. In other words, there is a tie between monogamy and happiness, and between promiscuity and depression. This correlation is much stronger for women than men. A young woman's likelihood of depression rose steadily as her number of partners climbed.

Another danger is relational. Sex outside marriage can overwhelm the relationship. Physical intimacy becomes a substitute for emotional intimacy. Electricity and stimulation gets confused with love and commitment. The sexual intimacy will dominate, which more often than not means that the infrastructure for a lasting relationship will not be built. According to the research of sociologists from the University of Chicago and the University of Michigan, couples who live together before marriage are more apt to have their marriage fail than those who move in together after their vows. Another study from the University of Wisconsin found that couples who cohabitate before marriage increase their odds of divorce by 50 percent, and only 15 out of every 100 cohabiting couples were married after a decade. What we've been led to believe is that if you live together first, you'll be better prepared for marriage, and therefore reduce the risk of divorce. It is a lie.

A final danger is the reduction of sex to that which is merely physical. In other words, the reduction of sex to lust. Lust takes the wonderful, beautiful gift of sex that God gave to men and women for their intimacy and pleasure within marriage, and makes it no more than an appetite, a desire, a physical craving to be filled. C. S. Lewis once said to think of the distortion of lust in this way:

> You can get a large audience together for a strip-tease act—that is, to watch a girl undress on the stage. Now suppose you came to a country where you could fill a theatre by simply bringing a covered plate on to the stage and then slowly lifting the cover so as to let every one see, just before the lights went out, that it contained a mutton chop or a bit of bacon, would you not think that in that country something had gone wrong with the appetite for food? And would not

anyone who had grown up in a different world think there was something equally queer about the state of the sex instinct among us?

God designed sex to be that which is given to another, shared with another, something that is a part of the deepest nature of community and intimacy. Lust is isolated, alone, reducing everything to an object, and only knows desire. It takes that which can deliver fulfillment and twists it into something that promises pleasure, but delivers only emptiness, because it rips it from its design. And sex as lust, taken into marriage, undermines its intimacy from the start.

## PORNOGRAPHY

There is one more area we should explore, and it is pornography. It really is the bane of this generation. When it comes to porn, the question facing many men and women is simple: is it really wrong? Is it really that big of a deal? I mean, it's just an image on a screen. It's not someone I know, or someone I'm having an actual affair with, so I'm still faithful to my future (or current) wife. It's just sexual release, like masturbation, and we all know that masturbation is not condemned in the Bible. It's not even mentioned. And isn't sex a good thing, so what's wrong in watching it happen? I'm just admiring beauty. And besides, I'm single, so what do you expect me to do with all this pent-up sexual energy? It seems like a safe release until I *am* married.

I've heard all of this, and more.

So is it really that big of a deal?

Yes, and here's why.

*It is sexual sin.* Jesus made it clear that when we give in to lust, it is akin to the act itself. It makes no difference whether you know the person or not; lust is not tied to relationship.

*It is addictive.* The ubiquitous nature of porn is new to our culture, and to human sexuality, but it is becoming increasingly clear that it is highly addictive in nature. As a result, it can not only begin to dominate a life, but can demand ever-increasing levels of exposure and ever-increasing degrees of experience to continue to stimulate.

*It is degrading to women.* In pornography, women are treated as objects. They are not fulfilling God's dream for their life as his precious daughter, nor are they fulfilling his design for sexual expression and fulfillment. You are watching a woman who is being sinned against, treated in a way that is contemptible to her heavenly Father (whether she sees it or not—and the fact that many may not only adds to its tragic nature). And if you are a woman watching it for the men, it is equally degrading to them.

*It leads to other sins.* Studies are beginning to show that the effects of porn on men are more than temporary sexual stimulation: as they see women treated as objects, they begin to treat women that way. They become more sexually aggressive, leading to date rapes and expected "hook-ups."

*It harms your relationship with your current, or future, spouse.* It is absolutely ridiculous to say that watching porn enhances a sexual life. Instead, it cheapens it. Those caught in its web testify to how porn quickly becomes a substitute for sexual intimacy with your spouse.

*It desensitizes your soul.* Sin of any kind desensitizes your spiritual life. Continued exposure to a sin such as pornography is like shooting Novocain into your soul. It deadens you and grieves the Holy Spirit in your life, forcing him to withdraw his utmost filling in a way that diminishes his power and presence in your life.

*It distorts sex.* Nothing reduces sex to lust more than pornography. Yielding to such images is overwhelmingly addictive, like a narcotic that delivers a quick hit to the emotions or senses, but ravages you from within. It destroys real relationships, real intimacy, real sexuality.

I'm a pastor. I talk with men who are dealing with the spiritual torment and guilt of engaging in pornography while trying to rationalize it away; I talk with men who are having to fight it as an addiction; I talk with men who are finding it is leading them to a warped view of women; I talk with men who are experiencing its direct path to other sins; I talk with men who are seeing its assault on their marriage; I talk with men who are trying to awaken their souls from its deadening grip; I talk with men who have distorted views of what sex is about. I also talk to the wives of these men— I've seen the hurt, the betrayal, the wounding to intimacy, trust and self-esteem. And increasingly, I am having the same conversations with women who have become caught in its snare. There is little doubt to those of us who work with people caught in its web, and those who are themselves caught, how pornography is destroying the sanctity of sex and the glory of marriage.

## SANCTA CAMISIA

So am I calling you to sexual purity? To virginity until marriage, and then fidelity within marriage? Of course. It is what holiness in your sexual life demands. If there is a sense where sexual sin carries greater spiritual harm, there is also a sense where sexual purity brings greater spiritual depth and intimacy with Christ. But rather than find this diminishing, it is enlarging. As Lauren Winner writes, "The *no* to sex outside marriage seems arbitrary and cruel apart from the Creator's *yes* to sex within marriage. Indeed, one can say that in Christianity's vocabulary the only real sex is the sex that happens in a marriage; the faux sex that goes on outside marriage is not really sex at all. The physical coming together that happens between two people who are not married is only a distorted imitation."

This brings to mind an item in the cathedral at Chartres that has beckoned pilgrims to its grounds for over a millennium. The cathedral has housed what tradition holds to be the tunic of the Blessed Virgin Mary, the *Sancta Camisia* or "Sacred Tunic," since 867. The tunic is the one be-lieved to be worn by the vir-gin when Christ was born. The relic was said to have been given to the cathedral by Charlemagne's grandson, Charles the Bald.

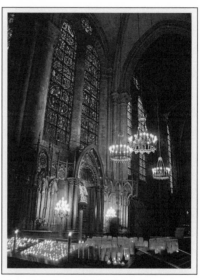

Though other shrines claimed similar relics, none had the seeming confirma-tion of as many miracles, chronicled in the *Miracles of Our Lady of Chartres*, an anonymous Latin manu-script of 1027. When a Nor-man Viking besieged the

Figure 5.3: Tango7174/Wikimedia Commons

city in 911, the bishop held up the *Sancta Camisia* on the walls of the city, then waving it like a banner, marched out to meet the enemy. It raised such fear and awe among the Vikings that they turned and fled. Not only that, the leader of the Viking raid (Raoul) made peace with the king (Charles III) and converted to Christianity, becoming the first Duke of Normandy.

But the greatest miracle of all took place when the cathedral was destroyed in 1194 and the sacred tunic was thought to be de-stroyed with it. Citizens throughout the city of Chartres felt aban-doned by God himself. As they searched through the rubble, the precious relic was recovered, unscathed, in the crypt of the church where it had been hidden away. It didn't hurt the symbolism of the event that it was found on the third day after the fire.

This was taken as a miraculous sign that not only was God with them, but that the church should be rebuilt even more magnificently than ever in honor of the mother of God. During its construction, "the town's inhabitants, from nobles to children, harnessed themselves to carts like beasts to haul the stones, and, it is said, tugged in silence, save for penitential prayers when they paused for rest."

How fitting that in a place built to remind us of the holy is a reminder of the sexual holiness of Mary from which Christ came.

And from which he has come to us.

# 6

## THE BILLY GRAHAM LIBRARY
## CHARLOTTE, NORTH CAROLINA

### YOU HAVE A CALLING

*That's the first thing I'm going to ask him when I get to heaven.*

BILLY GRAHAM, WHEN ASKED WHY GOD CHOSE TO USE HIM

✦ ✦ ✦

Figure 6.1: Used by permission of the Billy Graham Evangelistic
Association.

IT WAS IN MAY OF 1934 THAT Frank Graham lent a pasture to some thirty local businessmen who wanted to devote a day of prayer for Charlotte, North Carolina, because the depression had spread spiritual apathy throughout the city. During that day of prayer, out on the Graham land, their leader—Vernon Patterson—prayed that "out of Charlotte the Lord would raise up someone to preach the Gospel to the ends of the earth."

And the Lord did.

The great Anglican leader John Stott has written that "no single person in the twentieth century has been more influential for Christ than Billy Graham." Which is why I want to take you to a place devoted to his life, The Billy Graham Library in Charlotte, North Carolina. Designed the way presidential libraries are often fashioned, it is a moving experience, taking you not only through someone's life but through the main events of the twentieth century.

When you drive on to the museum's campus, you feel a sense of serenity, of peace, of calm. If you didn't know you were in Charlotte, you would think you were in the Blue Ridge Mountains of his beloved home in Montreat, North Carolina. Instead, you are at the place of his birth, which is why the main building is made to look like a barn at the dairy farm of his family.

Also on the site is a restoration of his boyhood home, and the place where he will be buried beside his beloved wife, Ruth. This is particularly moving for me personally as I was with Billy and Ruth at their home in Montreat just a few months before she died. At that time, I was deeply touched by his passionate love for her; I recall that following an hour or so of conversation, he walked us back to the bedroom where Ruth was confined to bed. She had gamely prepared to receive us, and had been moved to a nearby chair, next to a low-lying bookshelf where notebooks containing books of the Bible had been prepared for her with oversized type so that she could read them despite her failing eyesight. They talked of their nightly devotions with one another, how they prayed for their children and how those who said there was no romance at their age were wrong. "We have romance through our eyes," Billy explained. He was right. They did.

You may not have heard of Billy Graham. A recent study found that nearly one out of every three Americans under the age of thirty have not. Graham was a lanky North Carolina farm boy who felt called by God to the ministry of evangelism. Before his life would end, he would share the message of Jesus with more people—and see more of them respond—than any other figure in human history. And lest there be any doubt, a simple walk through the museum will make that clear.

The experience takes you through the eras of Graham's life and ministry, along with the history of our world that raced alongside. Through sight and sound and display, you are transported into the sawdust tents of revivals, the great Los Angeles

Figure 6.2: Used by permission of the Billy Graham Evangelistic Association.

crusade that launched a young Graham into the world's lime-
light, the Cold War and the Berlin Wall and his countless
opportunities to bring the gospel where it had never been openly
taken in his lifetime, stadiums filled with tens of thousands
eagerly listening to the message of Christ proclaimed with simplicity and power. It is, without a doubt, one of the most moving
exhibitions you will experience. Each room, each exhibit, brings
you into that time and place in ways that increasingly envelop
your spirit. You are not simply taken into this man's life, but into
his ministry, into his journey. Each time, and I have been on
several occasions, I walk away challenged to live more radically,
more passionately, more single-mindedly for Christ. I want nothing more than to model myself after Graham's life, a life that
pursued a calling from God and followed him out on that adven-
ture wherever it led.

By looking at his life, I want to talk about yours. Particularly,
*your* calling. Because you *have* been called—as strongly, and as
clearly, as Billy was called. Calling is a very simple idea that can be
made very complex. Let's see if we can simplify it—first, by looking at the great "calling" story in the Bible, the call of Abram, and
then how Billy embraced his call and made it his life.

## Story of Abram
The thing to note about the great call of Abram is that it was to *do*
something:

> The Lord had said to Abram, "Leave your country, your peo-
> ple and your father's household and go to the land I will
> show you.
>
>> "I will make you into a great nation
>>     and I will bless you;
>> I will make your name great,

> and you will be a blessing . . .
>   and all peoples on earth
>     will be blessed through you. . . ."

God said to him . . . "As for me, this is my covenant with you: You will be the father of many nations. No longer will you be called Abram; your name will be Abraham, for I have made you a father of many nations. I will make you very fruitful; I will make nations of you, and kings will come from you." (Genesis 12:1-3; 17:3-6)

Every life receives at least one call—and if the first one is answered, then comes a second call. The first of God's calls is to your heart to respond to Christ for forgiveness and leadership. This is the most foundational call of God on every life. Then, if that is answered, a second call comes. The second call on your life, relates to how Christ wants you to personally penetrate this world and live for him, making the difference he wants you to make. As with Abram, the second call often unfolds as part of a journey. We are given initial direction, but the specifics are revealed throughout our life. Let me share a bit of how this played out for me. When I became a follower of Christ at the age of twenty during my sophomore year in college, I remember walking back to my apartment, across our campus, the night of my decision. I knew that I had given my life fully; and for whatever reason, I knew that meant vocationally. I knew that I was going to devote my life, somehow, to the cause of Christ. I didn't know what that meant.

I didn't know what a lot of things meant.

When I got to my apartment, I woke up my roommate, "Brooksy," who was the shot-putter for our track team.

"Brooksy! Wake up! I became a Christian tonight!"

Rolling over, he sleepily said, "Does this mean we have to get rid of the beer?"

With equal enthusiasm, I said, "I don't know!"

At the time, I was a premed major in college. I wanted to be a doctor because it paid well. There was no sense whatsoever of it being a life God had called me to pursue. With my new life in Christ came a new sense of purpose. I wanted nothing more than to live the life that would make the most impact for him. If it was in medicine, fine, but if not, all the better. But as I evaluated medicine, through the lens of my newfound faith, it became clear that there was little to commend it. I was competent in science, but I didn't have a passion for medicine, a vision for what God would have me do with it. It simply wasn't who he made me to be.

I had been very involved in playing the guitar, singing and writing songs. I had won contests, and performed in some fairly large venues, and even recorded a demo tape of four of my songs. All of this turned instantly to Christ, and I naturally thought that might reflect the nature of my calling. Yet I grew increasingly uncomfortable with that sense of call; there was something ultimately unsatisfying about it for me. And let me hasten to add, for *me*. In truth, I was an artist, but not an *Artist*. Music was just one way the gift of creative communication was trying to bust out of my life. But it wasn't the singular way I was to use the gift. I could take you to the walkway by the science building at my school and show you the exact spot where the Spirit clearly impressed on me that the reason I was finding music increasingly vacuous was because I was not fundamentally a musician, or called to communicate to others optimally in that way.

But deep down, there was a growing sense of what I did have a passion for, what I was most able to do. Where I *could* make the most difference. What I *was* supposed to do. Was *made* to do.

I had always had an ability to teach, to package and communicate knowledge, to write. When I was in high school, I remember entering a public speaking contest through a business club just for kicks, and won it. Then I went to the regionals, and won it again. I was set to go the nationals, but there wasn't any money to send me. I later took a debate class, and found out that I could argue and reason effectively on my feet. In fact, I went undefeated.

But I just wrote off that kind of stuff. I never let such simple, basic understandings of who I was, and who God had made me to be, factor into my thinking about God's call on my life. Yet all of my life, that's what had been coursing through my veins as the deepest of passions and the strongest of abilities.

And I had always been a leader. Just not an intentional or focused one. Or very positive. I would lead the neighborhood kids into trouble; I would lead my elementary-school classes into open insurrection and rebellion. Later my leadership took a more constructive turn with roles in fraternities and student government, sports teams and music groups. But it never entered my mind that because I was a leader I should lead. Just as it had never occurred to me that because I was a communicator, I should communicate.

But the more I walked with Christ, and sought to give my life to him, the more those two areas of gifts and passion became my sense of true north. So after college I went to seminary to prepare for a life of leadership and communication in the only way I knew, which was through academia. I envisioned a life as a professor, writing and speaking in ways that I knew had influenced me as a college student. Once there, I accepted a seminary pastorate, and through that single step I fell in love with the church and had my ecclesiology awakened as to God's plan for its place in the Great Commission. My experience as a pastor showed me that my gifts in communication could be exercised in that arena as well. More importantly, it showed me that a pastoral role could combine my communication gifts with my leadership gifts. But I was still unsure if that was God's call.

After completing my Ph.D., I was offered two jobs—one with a small college as an assistant professor, and the other with a denomination as a leadership consultant. I went with the denominational role, as it seemed to offer a blend of the academy and the church. During that season more became clear; I was not a theoretician, but a practitioner. My vision expanded further regarding the church. Nineteen months later, I resigned to plant a church.

Through each step, the formative influences were an ever-deepening sense of the gifts God had given me, and how they could best be used, coupled with raw life experiences and opportunities that shaped my sense of calling along the way. Nearly fifteen years into it, when offered the opportunity to become the president of a seminary, I once again reopened my sense of God's calling, only to find that I truly was meant to serve the church as a pastor and to continue to be a writer. Looking back, everything I dreamed of pursuing has been achieved through this role. As I made my way through this life journey, I often felt unsure of each new step. What guided me throughout was my deep sense of my primary giftedness, and clear passions for ministry. Providence is always a doctrine best seen in retrospect; and looking back, the pursuit of my calling was served powerfully by God each step of the way.

## LISTENING TO YOUR CALL

So what is your second calling? Whatever it is, it is your life mission. This is what resonates throughout the Graham library. A person who was called to a mission, and then gave himself to it. You can't walk through the library and not answer the simplest of questions with the clearest of answers: What was Billy Graham's calling? Answer: evangelism. Even the library itself attempts to fulfill this calling, with an opportunity to respond at the end—as so many have before—to Graham's presentation of the gospel with a decision for Christ.

But when we talk about life mission, what we're really talking about is your vocation. No, not in the watered-down sense the world uses the term. The word "vocation" comes from the Latin word *vocatio*, or *vocare*, which means "summons" or "invitation." The dynamic behind vocation is that God calls us to himself so decisively that everything we are, everything we do, and everything we have is invested with a special devotion to him, as if we're living our life out as a response to his summons and service. In the twelfth chapter of Romans, the Bible says, "Take your everyday, ordinary life—your sleeping, eating, going-to-work, and walking-around life—and place it before God as an offering" (Romans 12:1 *The Message*). And in Colossians, it says, "Do your best. Work from the heart for your real Master, for God. . . . Keep in mind always that the ultimate Master you're serving is Christ" (Colossians 3:22-23 *The Message*).

We've lost the depth of that idea. Think of how we use the term *vocation*. We talk of "vocational education" and "vocational counseling," and when we say those things, we mean little more than job training and job placement. The heart of our calling, however, is not to some*thing*, but to *Someone*. The idea behind calling is that whatever our occupation may be, it is to be elevated to an expression of worship—as that which could be pleasing to God—if performed with excellence and integrity and heartfelt devotion. A real estate agent, then, is to represent her clients to the greater glory of God as a committed servant. A software developer's labor is to be infused with a sense of piety. A teacher should see himself on the front lines of what God is trying to do in this world.

But this is rare. Instead, Dorothy Sayers writes that we live in a world where "doctors practice medicine not primarily to relieve suffering, but to make a living. Lawyers accept briefs not because they have a passion for justice, but because the law is the profession that enables them to live." It's as if we have reduced being a

*Christian* doctor, or a *Christian* lawyer, to what is done outside of office hours in some form of "official" ministry setting—instead of seeing the practice of medicine or law as a ministry unto God.

But what, exactly, are you to pour yourself into in this way? If the idea of vocation is "calling," then there really is something there to listen to—something to follow. As Parker Palmer once wrote, "Before I can tell my life what I want to do with it, I must listen to my life telling me who I am." Or even more to the point, before I let God tell my life what he wants to do with it, I must listen to God telling me what my life is. And God will tell you; just not in the way you might think.

I once read something from the life of the ethicist John Kavanaugh. He went to work with Mother Teresa for three months at the "house of the dying" in Calcutta. He went not simply to serve, but to seek. He wanted a clear answer as to how best to spend the rest of his life. On the first morning there he met Mother Teresa. She asked him what she could do for him. Kavanaugh asked her to pray for him. She asked him what he wanted her to pray for. And he shared what had carried him thousands of miles from the United States.

He said, "Pray that I have clarity."

Her answer surprised him.

Very firmly, she said, "No. I will not do that."

He asked her why, and she said, "Clarity is the last thing you are clinging to and must let go of."

When Kavanaugh pointed out that she seemed to have clarity, she laughed, and said, "I have never had clarity; what I have always had is trust." Then she added, "So that is what I will pray for. I will pray that you trust God." And that was a good thing to pray for.

Just as my sense of call—particularly its specificity—unfolded over time through milestones and experiences and opportunities, so will yours. Countless lives never pursue, much less fulfill, their calling because they are waiting on clarity instead of acting on trust. They are waiting for the specificity of what God wants them to do, rather than the assurance that he will be with them and bring specificity as they journey together in relationship. They are wanting a road map, when he is wanting to come along as personal guide.

I answered my sense of God's call to full-time ministry before I knew what that meant; I went to seminary to prepare for a life of leading and communicating before I knew what that meant; I started a church before knowing all that it might hold for my life. I seldom had clarity; I always was offered the chance to trust.

That's the nature of answering God's call and joining in what he is doing in this world. It's not waiting on a detailed road map of what you are to do and when you are to do it. It's getting a sense of his call on your life, and being faithful with it—and seeking to please him with it, honor him with it, use it for him as much as you possibly can. Which means that the most profound "vocational" question is not the one we spend the most time on, which is "What should I do with my life?" Instead, it is the more foundational—and demanding—"Who am I?" and "How can I best serve God in light of who I am?" As Thomas Merton once wrote, "A tree gives glory to God by being a tree." And that's true—because God intended the tree to *be* a tree.

I have come late in my life to the work of Rainer Maria Rilke, drinking deeply from his well of poetry and reflection only over the last few years. A young man once wrote to ask Rilke if he should become a poet, and included a few lines of verse. Rilke responded:

> You ask whether your verses are any good. You ask me. You have asked others before this. You send them to magazines. You compare them with other poems, and you are upset

when certain editors reject your work. Now . . . I beg you to stop doing that sort of thing. You are looking outside, and that is what you should most avoid right now. No one can advise or help you—no one. There is only one thing you should do. Go into yourself. Find out the reason that commands you to write; see whether it has spread its roots into the very depths of your heart; confess to yourself whether you would have to die if you were forbidden to write. This most of all: ask yourself in the most silent hour of your night: *must* I write? Dig into yourself for a deep answer. And if this answer rings out in assent, if you meet this solemn question with a strong, simple "*I must*," then build your life in accordance with this necessity; your whole life, even into its humblest and most indifferent hour, must become a sign and witness to this impulse.

If you are an artist, you should pursue art.
If you are a teacher, you should teach.
If you are a leader, you should lead.
If you are a singer, you should sing.
If you are a children's worker, you should work with children.
If you are a scientist, you should pursue science.

How? That is what will make up much of your life journey. Don't worry about clarity. Instead, be faithful to who God made you to be, and seek to honor him with it. Let it become your all-consuming passion.

This is foreign language to our day, which only reveals our lost sense of calling. Here Rilke simply asks, "For what would you have to die if it were denied you . . . what *must* you do?" Rilke wisely adds this counsel:

I would like to beg you . . . to have patience with everything unresolved in your heart and to try to love the questions themselves as if they were locked rooms or books written in a very foreign language. Don't search for the answers, which could not be given to you now, because you would not be able to live them. And the point is, to live everything. Live the questions now. Perhaps then, someday, far in the future, you will gradually, without even noticing it, live your way into the answer.

Such convictions explain why I was so disturbed when I spent a week speaking to hundreds of college students from across several states at a camp in the mountains of Virginia. As I would linger and talk to the students over meals, I would ask them about their lives, and specifically what they planned to do with their majors. Most had no idea. And the thought of their major reflecting any sense of calling could not have been more alien to their thinking.

I remember asking a junior, "Why are you majoring in mechanical engineering?"

He said, "I don't know. I guess because I know I can get a job."

I instantly knew that if I had asked him, "Why do you want to get a job?" he would have said, "So I can make money."

And if I were to have asked him why he wanted to make money, he would have said, "So I can buy things, do things—so that I can live."

And if I were to have asked him why he wanted to live, he would have said, "So I can be happy."

And if I were to have asked him why he wanted to be happy, he would have said, "That's what life is about."

No, it is not. What life is about is who God made you to be, what he has called you to be, and the journey of trust over a lifetime that brings clarity in the end. God desires nothing more than

to infuse our heart and mind with a sense of meaning and purpose, and to call us to the front lines of what he is doing on this
planet in light of his divine plan for our place and role. If we don't
answer this call, we'll fill our lives with what will feel significant:
racing through our schedules, building a portfolio, climbing a ladder. But it won't be greatness. It won't be fulfillment. It won't be
destiny. We will be seduced into thinking it is, but it isn't. And as
a result, the world will stay the same, when we could have left the
one unique mark God created us to leave.

## Fulfilling Your Call

Yet talk of "calling" begs the question of "answering." Or even better, "fulfilling." I know, most would say, "If I knew God's call, of
course I would fulfill it!" That brings us back to thinking we need
clarity. Let's stay with trust. And even more importantly, faithfulness. All Christians receive a second call; why are so few used
mightily? It's because inherent within the second call is the need
for a personal resolve to be the person who can fulfill that call.

That's what set Graham apart. Known for his self-deprecation,
Graham was once asked why God chose to use him throughout the
world to introduce people to God. The evangelist responded, "That's
the first thing I'm going to ask him when I get to heaven." In truth,
we can get a glimpse of God's answer now. As I walked through the
museum dedicated to his life, it became clear that Graham's has
been a life marked by three things that enabled him to answer God's
call in the manner God dreamed of when the call was given.

*Integrity.* Once, when Graham was asked what one word he
wanted people to use when reflecting on his life, he said, "Integrity." I think he will get his wish. And there's a reason.

Early on, he gathered his young team around him in Modesto,
California, and hammered out their "Modesto Manifesto," com-
mitting themselves to financial integrity, moral purity and being

honest in all matters related to publicity. The commitment had teeth. Biographers have noted that during his ministry Graham has never had a meal alone with a woman other than his wife, Ruth, not even in a restaurant. He's never ridden in an automobile alone with a woman. Before he enters a hotel room, an assistant checks it out to make sure no woman is hiding in the closet or the bathroom or lurking behind the drapes, making him the victim of a setup. Once he is in the room, he will not answer the door unless he knows for certain who has knocked. Even into the last season of his life, on the rare occasions when only he and his secretary are in a room together, he keeps the door open wide. These are not the choices of a prude, but of a man who has determined what boundaries he needs to set in order to be a person of integrity.

Let's agree to follow his lead—perhaps not in specifics, but in principle, because fences of integrity around our life matter. Few people actually "fall" into sin; they creep into it, inch by inch, step by step, each one easily rationalized and innocent on the surface. And then, suddenly, they realize you have descended into a pit. And they don't want to be in the pit. Most of what I have experienced through God's grace and power has been a result of my personal integrity; that which has only been of the flesh or has resulted in a train wreck has been a result of my lack of integrity. It's a simple but powerful idea: the more you honor God, the more he will honor you.

And such integrity must not only be protected, but constantly cultivated. It must center your life from deep within. You may not be aware of how much Graham interacted with presidents. Early on, in his youthful enthusiasm, he chased after every opportunity to meet and pray with them in regard to their role. Over time, as he learned to distance himself from political liaisons, he became the one they chased after. One was Richard Nixon. Graham was deeply misled by Nixon throughout the Watergate affair. When he first read the transcripts from the Watergate tapes, he was so devastated that he not only wept, but vomited. That's how deeply, how viscerally, he felt the violation of an inherent sense of right and wrong in his heart. Historians take Graham to task for befriending Nixon in the first place; I hold him in high regard for his nausea.

Figure 6.3: Used by permission of the Billy Graham Evangelistic Association.

*Faithfulness.* A second reason why Graham's answer to God's call has impacted so many others revolves around faithfulness to the message of the Christian gospel. Early in his life, Graham wrestled with whether or not he was going to embrace the Bible as the inspired, revealed Word of God and therefore, the ultimate truth-source for his life, or view it through eyes that dismissed it as a fallible, unreliable book of merely human insight. He intuitively knew that this was no mere intellectual decision, but that it would alter the very trajectory of his life.

He had a friend named Chuck Templeton who, at the time, was facing the same decision. Both were rising stars in the evangelical world, although most considered Templeton the better speaker of the two. But as Templeton looked at the Bible, he made the conscious decision not to believe it, and to view it as little more than any other book. He then went to work on Graham to take a similar position.

The resolution came while Graham was at a student conference at Forest Home, a retreat center in the San Bernadino Mountains near Los Angeles. Graham went for a walk in the surrounding pine forest. About fifty yards off the main trail, he sat for a long time on a large rock that was there, with his Bible spread open on a tree stump. Then he made his choice, ultimately and finally, praying,

> Oh God, I cannot prove certain things. I cannot answer some of the questions Chuck is raising and some of the other people are raising, but I accept this Book by faith as the Word of God.

And that, Graham would later say, changed everything.

I've been to Forest Home, and on a similar walk, I accidentally stumbled on the very rock upon which Graham made his lifelong values choice. I knew it was the same rock, because there is now a bronze tablet on the stone, commemorating his decision. Why such recognition? Because it was through that decision that Graham was able to be used by God to change the world. Here's how Graham himself reflects on it:

> [That single resolution] gave power and authority to my preaching that has never left me. The gospel in my hands became a hammer and a flame. . . . I felt as though I had a rapier in my hands and through the power of the Bible was slashing deeply into men's consciousness, leading them to surrender to God.

Sadly, the world never heard any more from Chuck Templeton. He ended up resigning from the ministry, and eventually left the faith altogether. He was interviewed at the age of eighty-three, living with Alzheimer's disease. Asked by a journalist about his youthful decision, he reflected back on his life, and said that he missed Jesus. And then he broke down in tears, and could say no more.

I didn't know it at the time, but I now believe that one of the most formative moments in my spiritual life was when I was asked to participate in something that I sensed was unbiblical by someone very, very dear to me. I knew that if I said no, I would bring great emotional pain to this person, and to myself as well. It wouldn't be understood, and it could have ended our relationship. I was faced with a clear choice: obey my convictions, or disavow them for the sake of ease. It was the hardest decision I ever made, but a critical one. I stood by my convictions; when I did, it felt as if a sculptor tore away at the stone encasing my life, allowing me to become who God had called me to be.

You will have moments like this—moments where on the one hand you could follow the clear teaching of the Bible asking you to take a stand that may bring enormous pain and consequences, or on the other hand you could embrace compromise. How you choose *will shape* your call. And not just once, but every time you face such a decision. And trust me, you will face it over and over again.

*Passion.* But beyond the faithfulness, beyond the integrity, there is a third and final mark that will forever be a part of Graham's legacy: a life of single-minded passion. His passion was for a world that was lost apart from Christ.

Stephen Olford once reflected on visiting Graham on the top floor of the New Yorker hotel right before Graham's famed 1956 New York crusade. This was a crusade that would go down in history as one of the most important spiritual breakthroughs not only in Graham's ministry but for evangelical faith in America. He walked with him out on the balcony, and looking over the city, began to talk of the upcoming effort—about who would come, and how God might work. While they were talking, Stephen noticed that Graham began to break down in tears. He couldn't help it— he was crying over the city.

That passion is more critical than you might think. I've long observed that the natural flow of the human heart is toward itself, not toward others. At least I know that it works that way with mine. Let your passion flow outward toward others. Only then will what consumes you consume others.

In the summer of 2000 I joined thousands of other invited delegates to Amsterdam 2000, arguably Billy's last great leadership effort. It was an event that gathered evangelists from around the world in order to pass on the torch of passion that Billy and others of his generation have held so high. During one of the sessions, an interview was shown with a man who had come to the conference from Africa. He was a cheerful man, a happy man. He spoke of how much he had longed to come to Amsterdam to learn all that he could about sharing Christ with others, so that he could do everything possible to join with God on the mission. But he had no money to come. The price of the airline ticket, lodging and food was equal to an entire year's worth of food for him and his missionary family.

So this is what he did. He and his wife and family prayed, and decided together that going to Amsterdam to learn more about sharing Christ with a lost world was the most important investment they could make. That nothing was more critical than the building of the church—not just in Africa, but around the world— and that if this is what it took, it was worth whatever it took to get him there. They took their entire food allowance—the only money they were going to receive for food for the entire year—and spent it on sending him to Amsterdam so that he could become better at sharing Christ and building his church. He said that he had no idea what he would do, or how his family would eat. He ended by saying, "I believe Africa will never be the same." And you know what? I don't think it will.

## THE NEXT BILLY GRAHAM

It is often asked, "Who will be the next Billy Graham?" The answer, of course, is no one. The real question is who will carry on Graham's integrity, Graham's faithfulness and Graham's passionate sense of mission? Because that is the torch he carried, and the torch that he has to pass. Graham himself shares that he is often reminded of the story he once heard in India about Mahatma Gandhi, who allegedly said, "I would become a Christian if I could have seen one." In Billy Graham, the world finally saw one.

In his closing words to those of us in Amsterdam, conveyed by satellite from his bed at the Mayo Clinic, Graham told of the famed Christian martyrs, Nicholas Ridley and Hugh Latimer, who were burned at the stake for their Christian beliefs. Just before his death, Latimer uttered a cry which has echoed across the centuries: "Be of good comfort, Master Ridley, and play the man! We shall this day light such a candle, by God's grace, in England, as I trust never shall be put out."

The story was particularly compelling to me, having come to the Netherlands from a time of study at Oxford, where I had seen the site where those two men were killed for their faith. Graham then challenged us to light a fire in our generation that, by God's grace, would never be put out. He called us to hold the light of our lives high so that all the world could see the One we proclaim Lord and Savior, Jesus the Christ, as the very Light of the World.

I wrote earlier in this chapter about a special day I spent with Billy Graham at his home in Montreat, North Carolina, along with his precious wife, Ruth, just a few months before she died. I was in the presence of a man who assumed and fulfilled God's call as few others have in the history of the world. I was not struck by the clarity of his call, but by his trust and faithfulness to its inherent claim on his life. He knew he was an evangelist; how that played out was God's domain, but he was to be an evangelist. That simple idea guided his entire life. Not crusades, not stadiums, just a sense of who God made him to be and the man God called him to be.

And you are called to be . . . well, you.

And to be faithful to it.

And that's all.

# 7

# Lutherstadt-Wittenberg, Germany

## YOU CAN MAKE HISTORY

*A wild boar has invaded thy vineyard.*

Written against Luther and presented to the pope

✦ ✦ ✦

Figure 7.1: Cethegus/Wikimedia Commons

IT WAS 1521. A MAN BY THE NAME of Martin Luther stood in front of the Holy Roman Emperor, along with an array of other leaders representing the religious and political establishment of the day, to answer charges of heresy. "Martin, how can you assume that you are the only one to understand the sense of scripture? Would you put your judgment above that of so many famous men and claim that you know more than they all?" pressed the brilliant Catholic theologian Johann von Eck. "I ask you, Martin, answer candidly . . . do you or do you not repudiate your books and the errors which they contain?"

The words poured, first from his heart, and then from his lips in his native German: "Unless I am convicted by Scripture and plain reason—I do not accept the authority of popes and councils, for they have contradicted each other—my conscience is captive to the Word of God. I cannot and I will not recant anything, for to go against conscience is neither right nor safe. God help me. Here I stand, I cannot do otherwise. Amen."

Martin Luther was born in Saxony in 1483. Schooled in Erfurt, he later fled to an Augustinian monastery. Literally. Caught in a thunderstorm, in terror before the lightning, he cried out, "Help, St. Anne, I will become a monk!" Despite this less than auspicious beginning, from that point on Martin Luther was a man of the church. And from this man of the church came the greatest reformation of the church in history.

The Protestant Reformation of the sixteenth century which altered the course of Western history in seismic fashion.

By any account, Martin Luther must rank as one of the most influential European figures of the last millennium. Marco Polo and Columbus opened up new continents, Shakespeare and Michelangelo produced some of the most sublime pieces of art, and Napoleon and Hitler changed the political face of their centuries. Yet Luther and the Reformation he triggered have made a huge impact not just on Europe, but . . . throughout the rest of the world. Protestantism shaped a whole new way of life for countless people across the Western world and beyond, which coloured their approaches to God, work, politics, leisure, family—in fact, almost every aspect of human life . . . [including] the early development . . . of the United States, and . . . the emergence of democracy and economic and religious freedoms in Europe.

And to think it all started with this simple monk nailing ninety thoughts on a church door in Wittenberg, Germany.

The Reformation was more than theological; it was *ecclesiastical*. It was a reformation of the *church*. Even the famed Ninety-Five Theses nailed onto the Wittenberg door say nothing about justification by faith, the authority of the Bible, the priesthood of all believers or any of the other well-known Reformation doctrines. Instead, they look like a treatise on church practice. And for Luther's day, this meant a treatise on life itself. And it was revolutionary: Luther's ultimate vision for reformation was for a church where each member could play an active and decisive part, the distinction between clergy and laity could be dissolved and every believer be seen as a priest, and thus be able to powerfully "espouse the cause of the faith" to a lost and dying world.

Luther encouraged his fellow monks to break out of the monasteries and walk among those in the world. Once there, he encouraged those in the world to see their place in life as deeply "called" as those of the monks, and to take their place in the church's enterprise as fellow ministers.

In essence, Martin Luther felt anyone could, and everyone should, make history with their life.

## THE WRONG WAY TO WITTENBERG

I really want you to go to Wittenberg. You can see almost all of the historic area on a one-mile stretch of Collegienstrasse and Schlossstrasse that begins at the railroad tracks and ends at the Schlosskirche (Castle Church). The church itself is simple enough; a fire tore through it in 1760, destroying such things as the wooden doors on which Luther nailed his Ninety-Five Theses. Inside is a simple tomb marking Luther's burial spot, as well as his writing partner, Melanchthon. Nearby is the Luther House and Museum, located in the Augustinian monastery where Luther lived as a monk and then later with his family. A wonderful time to go is during Luthers Hochzeit (Luther's Wedding), the city festival that commemorates and reenacts Luther's marriage to Katharina von Bora. It's the second weekend of June, and the city goes back in time to 1525 with period costumes and entertainment.

Just don't do it the way I did. The first time I tried (that already tells you a lot, doesn't it?), I flew into Frankfurt, then made the connection to Berlin. No problem.

But then the bus from the Berlin airport that was to take me to the main train station in seven minutes took twenty. This made catching the train to Wittenberg that I had hoped for impossible. When I got to the station for my intended "day" trip, I looked for a locker to store my luggage. No luck. I looked for thirty minutes, and all were filled. Time was running out, and I was getting frantic. Only by chance did I stumble upon a concierge storage service that I didn't even know existed.

Now I was forced to take a second, later train to Wittenberg. I was sleepy, tired and already frustrated that my one day set aside for my visit was slipping away (I had to fly to London the next morning). As I sat on the second train, I thought to myself how unimpressive the landscape looked. No worries; I was going to go where Protestantism began, where the one and only Martin Luther served as a professor and pastor while an Augustinian monk, where he later nailed to the door of the Castle Church his Ninety-Five Theses in protest of the medieval church's abuses. Who cared about the scenery?

When I arrived, now approaching 1 p.m., I quickly moved to a nearby "tourist" map of the city, posted on a board by the rail station, so that I could acclimate myself and get a sense of where to walk, as I had no time to waste. But there wasn't a single recognizable landmark. Not a single street name that I had come prepared to look for; no famous locations; *nothing was there.* I must have stared at it for fifteen minutes. Assuming I just needed some help, I spotted two women nearby staffing some kind of welcome table. I asked them if they spoke English—they didn't—but between my pass-the-test-and-move-on graduate school German and their broken English, we collectively ascertained what I was looking for.

"This is Wittenberge, not Wittenberg," one of the women tried helpfully to say (you'll notice the "e" at the end of the first name).

In my amazing grasp of the obvious, I said, "There's another Wittenberg?"

That didn't quite compute. So I tried again.

"I'm in the wrong place?"

The word *wrong* worked.

"Yes" they said, "Wrong place."

So where in Germany was I?

Still not sure we were understanding each other, I tried one more bit of broken German, asking where "Lutherhaus" was.

Then they said, in equally broken English, "Luther not here."

"He's not here?"

"No, Luther not here."

At that point—my one and only day for a long-desired pilgrimage almost gone, hot, frustrated, stressed from missed trains and racing against time, jet lagged, no sleep—I wanted to say, "Then where in the **** is he?!"

Now that's a good pastor resting on study break for you. And far from the most inspired of responses in regard to a sixteenth-century dead guy. Before she could answer my imaginary question, I went running—seriously, a dead flat run I hadn't done since my old basketball days—to find the ticket office as I now had only minutes to catch the 1:12 train back to Berlin and try to salvage the day. Of course, there was a line, and when it finally dwindled to two, the woman directly in front of me was asking every conceivable question known to man—well, woman. I seriously think I heard her ask about the agent's shoes.

Finally, needing only one quick bit of information, I broke in and said, "What platform is the 1:12 train?" It was already 1:10. The agent looked shocked that I had broken in (cementing the pushy American stereotype), but then told me it was platform three, so I then ran, sweating, and caught the train. A minor victory to a sucky day. I had an hour and twenty minutes to fume on the way back to Berlin and to think through how to get to my destination. When I arrived, I went immediately to the ticket station to see if I had any chance at all of getting to the real Wittenberg, which I discovered is actually named "Lutherstadt-Wittenberg." There I was with a Ph.D. in Christian theology and history, and I had never, ever heard the famed city referred to as anything but just plain old Wittenberg. Not in any book, lecture, article—nothing. Consider that oversight now corrected.

With time running out, I ran through the station to the ticket counter to get a ticket to the real Wittenberg, and there must have been fifty people in line. Who were these people? I took my place in line. Suddenly, I glanced over and saw a first-class line with no people. I was ready to fork over any amount of cash to get *somewhere* that day. I broke out of the queue, walked quickly over, only to have the agent see me coming and immediately put up the "closed" sign as I approached. I wheeled around, and took my place back in line by glowering at the diminutive Asian man who had been behind me and had quickly filled my space. This was not the day to mess with me.

When my turn for an agent finally came, I asked her if she spoke English. She proudly told me she was the only one of the ticket agents who did not. Again, I used my broken German—and she her prized almost non-existent English—to arrive at the fact that my desired day was not going to take place. The next train was only minutes away (no way to make it in time), and it wouldn't get me to Wittenberg until after Luther's home and the famed church that posted his theses was closed. So it was over to claim my luggage, out to get a taxi, across town to the hotel and then up to my room. But not before saying to myself, at the end of it all, "I think this is

when people say they need a beer." Thankfully, I was in Germany, the home of Oktoberfest and beer gardens. Luther, who imbibed freely, was probably looking down and smiling.

But in many ways, my journey was his journey. When he set out to post his Ninety-Five Theses on the door of the Witten-berg church, he never thought it would lead him to an audience be-

Figure 7.2: AlterVista/Wikimedia Commons          fore the Holy Roman Emperor to answer charges of heresy. He never would have dreamed that something we now call the Protestant Reformation would be born. He never would have envisioned the end of the monolithic hold of Roman Catholicism on Europe, much less the myriad denominations and sects that sprang into existence, and not at all that one of them would bear his name.

This is what brings so many pilgrims to see his church, his home and a door where he posted one of the first viral blogs. Yes, there was much in place politically that served the chain of events that erupted from his life; yes, Luther was a good writer and theologian. But we come to absorb a singular life that ended up making history, and to remember how he did it.

And how did he do it?

It was the number he picked.

## Picking a Number

In 1998, two graduate students at Stanford picked a number. It was the number googol, which is a one followed by one hundred zeroes. That was how much information they dreamed of cataloging for their Internet search engine. To keep that dream in front of them, they named their company "Google." Now there are tens of millions of searches through Google every day, accessing billions of pages in nearly a hundred languages, and the term "googling" has now become synonymous with Web surfing.

While Google is a great search engine, that isn't what made the difference. It's not why they've become such a big part of our culture. It was the number they picked. Because that number wasn't just a number—it was a dream—and they decided to make it a big one. But it wasn't just a dream—the number was also a sense of resolve. A commitment. A determination. A sense of what they were going to strive for.

What Luther had, in great measure, was faith. Indeed, it was the foundation of his theological life and of the Reformation itself: we are saved by grace, through faith, not works. Luther had faith in a salvation rooted in God, not himself.

It translated into how he lived life itself. And rightfully so. Faith is a critical component of being used by God. His first followers tried to make the impact Jesus made, tried to do the wonderful works he achieved, tried to be the light he called them to be, and failed. So they asked him why, and he told them: "You're not yet taking God seriously. . . . The simple truth is that if you have a mere kernel of faith, a poppy seed, say, you would tell this mountain, 'Move!' and it would move. There is nothing you wouldn't be able to tackle" (Matthew 17:20-21 *The Message*). And then, two chapters later, he would add these unforgettable words: "With God all things are possible" (Matthew 19:26).

And as if there were any doubt what Jesus wanted to get across, two chapters later, we encounter one of the most provocative scenes in the New Testament:

> Jesus was returning to the city. He was hungry. Seeing a lone fig tree alongside the road, he approached it anticipating a breakfast of figs. When he got to the tree, there was nothing but fig leaves. He said, "No more figs from this tree—ever!" The fig tree withered on the spot, a dry stick. The disciples saw it happen. They rubbed their eyes, saying, "Did we really see this? A leafy tree one minute, a dry stick the next?"
>
> But Jesus was matter-of-fact: "Yes—and if you embrace this kingdom life and don't doubt God, you'll not only do minor feats like I did to the fig tree, but also triumph over huge obstacles. This mountain, for instance, you'll tell, 'Go jump in the lake,' and it will jump. Absolutely everything, ranging from small to large, as you make it a part of your

believing prayer, gets included as you lay hold of God." (Matthew 21:18-22 *The Message*)

And if that doesn't move you out of your comfort zone, we have these words of Jesus recorded by the apostle John: "The person who trusts me will not only do what I'm doing but even greater things, because I . . . am giving you the same work to do that I've been doing. You can count on it. From now on, whatever you request along the lines of who I am and what I am doing, I'll do it. . . . I mean it. Whatever you request in this way, I'll do" (John 14:12-14 *The Message*).

What's the headline? It's simple: There really is a God. When we align ourselves with him, pray to him, join with him in what he is doing, God-things happen. C. S. Lewis once observed that the New Testament contains what can only be called embarrassing promises of what prayer can unleash. It's true. They border on the scandalous. But most of us don't believe in that God. We don't pray to that God. We aren't in relationship with that God.

And that, Jesus said, is the problem. This isn't a "name it, claim it" approach to life. This isn't about working up enough belief, and then you call on God like he's some kind of cosmic errand boy or genie who has to do your will because you rubbed the bottle just right. And it's not about being entitled to a privileged life, a life heralded by others as worthy of acclaim. Becoming a maker of history is not about fame. It's about joining with God to advance the kingdom of God and bring God glory. Jesus was very clear: "*Whatever you request along the lines of who I am and what I am doing, I'll do it.*" If you want to experience God—if you want to see mountains move—then find out what God is doing, and join him. The question is the degree to which you will join him.

## How Many Arrows?

There is an obscure little passage in the Old Testament, tucked
away in the book of 2 Kings, that tells of the death of the great
prophet Elisha. Between the last reference to the life of Elisha, and
this story of his death, there is a forty-three-year period of silence.
So the events surrounding his death were apparently deemed important enough to God to ensure that they were recorded.

Elisha was suffering from an illness, and the king of Israel went
to see him. Seeing Elisha on his deathbed, the king suddenly realizes that Elisha, as a prophet of God, has been the key to Israel's
military success—over and over again—even more so than the
military itself! He suddenly sees that without God involved, there
could be no hope of gaining ground, of going further.

In response, Elisha gives the king a final opportunity for his
blessing in relation to building the kingdom. He tells the king to
get a bow and some arrows, and has him take the bow and arrows
in his hand. Then Elisha put his hands on the king's hands. When
he does that, he is making it clear that what he is about to do will
be full of spiritual symbolism and significance and blessing.

Here's the story:

Elisha said, "Get a bow and some arrows," and he did so.
"Take the bow in your hands," he said to the king of Israel.
When he had taken it, Elisha put his hands on the king's
hands.

"Open the east window," he said, and he opened it.
"Shoot!" Elisha said, and he shot. "The Lord's arrow of vic-
'tory . . . ," Elisha declared. (2 Kings 13:15-17)

In order to make sure that the king knew that what God would
do would be linked to what he was willing to do, he then said,
"Now, take the arrows, and strike the ground." Meaning that he
was to take the remaining arrows, and shoot them not out the

window as a sign of calling on what God would do, but at the ground, reflecting what he was willing to do. Symbolic of his willingness to take up the task at hand, to join with what God was willing and wanting to do through him.

Again, the Scriptures:

> Then he said, "Take the arrows," and the king took them. Elisa told him, "Strike the ground." He struck it three times and stopped. The man of God was angry with him and said, "You should have struck the ground five or six times; then you would have defeated [your enemy] and completely destroyed [him]. But now you will defeat [him] only three times." (2 Kings 13:18-19)

Then Elisha died and was buried.

That little story has stuck with me for a very long time. The king was given an opportunity for blessing, a chance to join with what God was willing to do. Everything was in place. There was a God of wonders ready to work wonders. The king believed in what God could do (that's why he went to Elisha in the first place). He was clearly aligned with God's will in terms of establishing the kingdom of Israel against its enemies.

So where did it all break down? The number he picked. What he was willing to do. In striking the ground three times, he revealed he was only moderately enthusiastic about it all. He was only willing to go so far, to extend himself so much, to invest in what it would take to move forward in only a limited way. He had more arrows that could have been shot, but he took it upon himself to only shoot three. But by only shooting the ground three times, not even using everything at his disposal, he revealed the lack of zeal, the lack of commitment, he had for giving everything he had to the accomplishment of the mission. He didn't do everything he could. And that caused God to withhold his full hand of blessing, the full measure of what he was willing and able to do.

Making history actually has less to do with you and your abilities than it does with your faith in God and his abilities. It's easy to think of Luther as simply a great man, and he was. But you, too, are a great person. Yet the real story is our great God.

When God prompted him to act, Luther didn't post five theses, or even twenty-five theses, but ninety-five of them—a sweeping critique that laid out a vision for a different church. Luther seized his moment and made history. In your life, you will have countless opportunities presented to you, by God, to do something significant in this world with your life. At various points and times, God will inject moments into the ebb and flow of your life to do something life-changing, even world-changing. These will be moments in time that are divine in nature, supernatural in potential and eternal in significance. The Bible even has a word for them—they are called "kairos" moments.

This is an idea that is often lost in our world, but it was keenly felt in ages past. The ancient Greek language had two principal words for time. One was *chronos*, where we get our word "chronological." This referred to calendar time—days, weeks, months, years. Then they had a second word for time—*kairos*—a word that meant something radically different. Something deeper. In truth, we don't even have an English equivalent for it. Kairos has to do with the quality of time. It's a moment pregnant with eternal significance and possibility. It's a moment when we are confronted with a choice, or decision, or potential action that holds the deepest level of significance for who we are, who we are becoming, and what our life impact will be.

This sense of time filled with opportunity runs deep throughout the biblical materials. For example, when the prophet Jeremiah talked about the life of the great Pharaoh of Egypt, he spoke of him as being a king who was only a loud noise, and nothing more, because he had missed his kairos—he had missed his moment. And then there is the scene toward the end of Jesus' life where he comes to a ridge overlooking the city of Jerusalem, and the Bible says that he breaks down and weeps. Why? Because they did not recognize the time—the kairos—of God's coming to them. In many ways, your entire life on this planet is a kairos moment. The question is whether you will see the opportunity of it that God has brought your way.

## CONVICTION AND COURAGE

This is why any attempt to make a pilgrimage to Wittenberg is worthwhile: to remember the power of a single life to make history. A life that seized its kairos moment. And how he did it is critical to remember: not simply through a large vision, but a vision coupled with *conviction* and *courage*.

The impetus behind the posting of Luther's Ninety-Five Theses on October 31, All Saints' Eve, in 1517 is worth remembering. It was the sale of indulgences. An indulgence was the pardon granted by the church of the punishment due a person from their already forgiven sins. In essence, it borrowed from the storehouse of merit earned by Jesus and the saints. The idea was that the head of the church was in charge of this

Figure 7.3: Selling indulgences to Catholics in the Middle Ages. Used by permission of Art Resource, NY.

storehouse of kitchen-passes. In Luther's time, the granting of indulgences was "vulgarized and commercialized by mountebanks and professional pardon-peddlers."

Like Johannes Tetzel. Tetzel worked Luther's part of the world, and it pushed Luther over the edge. All one had to do was pay a certain sum, and you would receive a full escape from any punishment in purgatory. No confession needed. You could even arrange to buy such an indulgence for a friend already there.

One could imagine how Tetzel's pitch pushed young Martin over the edge:

When a coin in the coffer rings,
a soul from purgatory springs.

Posting something on the door of a church, a glorified bulletin board, seems mild by most standards. It was also relatively common for the day, a regular feature of University life, and the typical way of giving notice for debate. And the University of Wittenberg itself was a relatively obscure institution in a rather small town of dirty streets and mud houses with straw roofs.

But it was born of conviction, which led to courage, and that is what God used. And it took courage; by taking on indulgences, Luther would end up taking on the church. This was not envisioned by Luther (thesis number seventy-one of his famed ninety-five supported the proper use of indulgences). Yet it would be this courage, fueled by his conviction, that propelled Luther step by step from the abuse of indulgences to an indictment of the entire confessional system and, in the end, the Protestant Reformation. As the novelist Elizabeth Rundle Charles has Luther maintaining:

If I profess with the loudest voice and clearest exposition every portion of the truth of God except precisely that little point which the world and the devil are at the moment attacking, I am not confessing Christ, however boldly I may be professing Christ. Where the battle rages, there the loyalty of the soldier is proved and to be steady on all the battle front besides, is mere flight and disgrace if he flinches at that point.

When people talk about making history, they tend to think of it in terms of personal fulfillment or fame. Seldom do they think in terms of impact, or in regard to confronting something enormously evil with the greater power of good at great personal risk to themselves.

As I write these words, the world's eyes have been turned toward Cairo. A revolution has taken place with stunning speed; in a handful of days an autocratic leader in power for over three decades has been removed. The genesis of the uprising has been widely seen as the convergence of three factors that together made up a "perfect storm" of revolution: (1) a large population of young people (today the Arab world has over 100 million people between the ages of 15 and 29); (2) widespread poverty and unemployment; and (3) the availability of social media, such as Twitter, Facebook and texting for communication and organization.

I was in Cairo just eight months earlier than the events that captured the world's attention. Not only was I in Tahrir (now "Liberation") Square, but traveled extensively throughout the country. Though nothing at that time signaled that an immediate uprising was to come, I can attest to the abject poverty and overwhelmingly challenging economic conditions that faced so many of the people who lived there. That revolt came was not surprising; that it came so quickly was. And from that one revolution came many others throughout the Middle East.

The word that was shouted throughout Egypt was *Kefaya!*—an Egyptian Arabic word (slang, actually) that means "enough." While this is the unofficial name of a grassroots political reform movement in Egypt, the word took on a far wider and deeper meaning. It became a cry of anger, of despair—and of determination. Young people in the region had enough of being ignored. Enough of being abused. Enough of being silenced. Enough of being forgotten. Enough of being left behind as the rest of the world rushed ahead.

So what will you be willing to say "enough" to? Will you see your one and only life effect political, social or, dare you dream it, spiritual change? Even if it means danger? Even death?

## FEELING UNWORTHY

Of course, all this talk about making history may make you feel a bit intimidated. Or even more likely, simply unworthy. It reminds me of a game that psychotherapist and author Larry Crabb once wrote about; a group therapist would play a game with people in his groups called "Top Secret." Here's how the game worked. He would ask them to write out the one thing about themselves that they were the least inclined to share, and to then return the paper unsigned. In other words, write down the one thing that nobody knows about you—the one thing you've never shared. Over the years, one answer has consistently emerged as the most frequently admitted top secret: "I feel utterly worthless."

When we are real, open, vulnerable—willing  to be truthful with ourselves and the world—what we admit is that we do not consider ourselves of much real value. Luther felt the same way. In 1527, he wrote, "For more than a week I was close to the gates of death and hell. I trembled in all my members. Christ was wholly lost." This reached a point of spiritual crisis, with Luther writing that "the content of the depressions was always the same, the loss of faith that God is good and that he is good to me."

So what made the difference? Luther insisted on listening to an-other, more important, voice. The voice of the truth of God's Word, over and against his own insecurities, doubts and misgivings. Even over the accusing voice of the evil one. He tells of how the devil approached him one day and accused him of the enormous sin in his life. Satan laid out a long list of sins of which Luther was guilty, and thrust them under his nose in accusation. Luther said to the devil, "Think a little harder; you must have forgotten some." So the devil thought a little harder and added another few hundred to the list. When the devil was finished, Luther said, "Okay, now take a pen and some red ink and write across that list 'The blood of Jesus Christ, God's Son, cleanses us from all sin.'"

You can take up the same pen, writing as Luther himself did in his magnificent hymn "A Mighty Fortress Is Our God," the title now etched around the tower of Castle Church,

> And though this world, with devils filled,
> should threaten to undo us,
> we will not fear, for God hath willed
> his truth to triumph through us.
> The Prince of Darkness grim,
> we tremble not for him;
> his rage we can endure,
> for lo, his doom is sure;
> one little word shall fell him.

## THE GREAT ROAD

I suppose everything I am writing in this chapter is to keep you away from the seduction of making your life less than it is by filling it with things that feign importance. God desires nothing more than to infuse your heart and mind with a sense of meaning and purpose, and to call you to the front lines of what he is doing on this planet in light of his divine plan for your place and role.

Your mission, your place, will be unique from all others. He has a vision for your life that is yours and yours alone. If you don't answer the call, you'll fill your life with what will feel significant:

racing through your schedule, building a portfolio, climbing a ladder. But it won't be greatness. It won't make history.

But if you answer the call of God, and walk with him in obedience, submission and devotion, if you give your life over to him—then you will become who you were created to be. And you will do incredible things. Because God is a big God, who wants to do big things—and he wants to do them through us—and for us to want to do them with him.

So many people have seen the deservedly acclaimed movies based on J. R. R. Tolkien's *Lord of the Rings* that I fear ever fewer will ever turn its magical pages. The books are so much richer, and the story so much deeper, than film could ever portray (though I love the films!). In reminiscing about Bilbo Baggins, his uncle, young Frodo recalls how

> he used often to say there was only one Road; that it was like a great river: its springs were at every doorstep and every path was its tributary. "It's a dangerous business, Frodo, going out of your door," he used to say. "You step into the Road, and if you don't keep your feet, there is no telling where you might be swept off to."

People who make history take that first step on to the Road. They do *something*. In many ways, as you stand before the door of the church where Luther posted his Ninety-Five Theses, that's what comes home. He had no idea of the Road before him; he had no idea what God would do with his courage and conviction.

But he did *something*.

Our first thought is not about what we have to do, but about what's been done to us, and because of that, what someone should do for us. Our tendency is to expect something to enter into our world and change things. We seldom think that we are already in the world to be that agent of change.

# 8

## Ten Boom House
## Haarlem, Holland

### YOU CAN TRUST GOD'S WILL

*Lord Jesus, I offer myself for Your people.*
*In any way. Any place. Any time.*

CORRIE TEN BOOM

✦ ✦ ✦

Figure 8.1: Jane023/Wikimedia Commons

"A ticket to Haarlem, please." My Dutch wasn't very good, but the person behind the window in the Amsterdam train station understood the name of the city, and soon I was on my way to the house of Corrie ten Boom and her family.

I was unashamedly on a pilgrimage.

In the late 1930s, Corrie was an elderly woman living in a small town in the Netherlands, better known as Holland. Her home, called the Beje (pronounced bay-yay), was a tilting, centuries-old house in the center of Haarlem and its bumpy brick streets. Its name came from children who visited the house who were unable to pronounce the name of the street on which it was found, Bartelijorisstraat.

Actually, it was two houses. In Corrie's own words, "In front was a typical tiny old-Haarlem structure, three stories high, two rooms deep, and only one room wide. At some unknown point in its long history its rear wall had been knocked through to join it with the even thinner, steeper house in back of it—which had only three rooms, one on top of the other." Squeezed between the two was a narrow corkscrew staircase. The family used a side door which opened out onto a tiny alleyway and led to a workroom. Corrie's father, a watchmaker, maintained a small watch shop in a room fronting the street. The Beje was so closed in by the houses around that the window plants that Corrie's sister Betsie planted each spring never grew tall enough to bloom.

Horrified by the German onslaught against the Jewish people of her country, Corrie—along with her family—began to hide those most threatened by arrest within their home. It was precisely the eccentric design and construction that allowed such a perfect "hiding place" to be built in Corrie's bedroom. To this day, you can tour her home and see the wall behind which so many Jewish persons were hidden, protected from capture and, most certainly, death.

She was eventually discovered, and was sent first to a prison in Vught built by German occupying forces for political prisoners.

Soon, she was transported deep within Germany to a place whose very name struck terror, Ravensbrück, the notorious extermination camp. Her father died within the first two weeks of his arrest. Corrie and her sister lasted through Vught, and then Ravensbrück, where her sister eventually died. Corrie survived. The humiliation, the beatings, the deprivation, the starvation, the sickness, the stench—she survived. Released on a clerical error a week before she was scheduled to enter the ovens, Corrie spent the rest of her life speaking of Christ's love and forgiveness, mercy and sustenance, goodness and trustworthiness, wherever she went. Eventually her story was captured in the bestselling book *The Hiding Place*, one of the most life-changing biographies you will ever read. Corrie became an ambassador to the world. She also became, to me, a mentor for many of life's most pressing issues.

It's why I came to her house in Haarlem. To see the "hiding place." And perhaps most of all, to remember what it means to trust God.

Corrie learned to trust early through the faith of her family. When she witnessed the death of a baby as a young girl, she realized that death could come to anyone. That night she burst into tears and sobbed to her father, "I need you! You can't die! You can't!"

Her father sat down on the edge of her narrow bed. "Corrie," he began gently, "when you and I go to Amsterdam—when do I give you your ticket?"

She sniffed a few times, considering his words.

"Why, just before we get on the train."

"Exactly. And our wise Father in heaven knows when we're going to need things, too. Don't run out ahead of him, Corrie. When the time comes that some of us will have to die, you will look into your heart and find the strength you need—just in time."

His words would be proven over and over. For example, the barracks where she and her sister Betsie were placed in Ravensbrück were terribly overcrowded and flea-infested. They had been able to miraculously smuggle a Bible into the camp, and in that Bible they had read that in all things they were to give thanks, and that God can use anything for good. Corrie's sister Betsie decided that this meant thanking God for the fleas. This was too much for Corrie, who said she could do no such thing. Betsie insisted, so Corrie gave in and prayed to God, thanking him even for the fleas.

Over the next several months a wonderful, but curious, thing happened. They found that the guards never entered their barracks. This meant that women were not assaulted. It also meant that they were able to do the unthinkable, which was to hold open Bible studies and prayer meetings in the heart of a Nazi concentration camp. Through this, countless numbers of women came to faith in Christ. Only at the end did they discover why the guards had left them alone and would not enter into their barracks.

It was because of the fleas.

Such lessons in trust shaped Corrie's life. After her time as a prisoner in Ravensbrück, she traveled throughout the world telling her story of suffering in the context of her love for God. Such were her wanderings that she referred to herself as a "tramp for the Lord." For thirty-three years following Ravensbrück, she never had a permanent home. When she was eighty-five years old, some friends provided her with a lovely home in California. It was a luxury she never dreamed she would have. One day, as a visitor was leaving, he said, "Corrie, hasn't God been good to give you this beautiful place?" She replied firmly, "God was good when I was in Ravensbruk, too."

Trusting in God is an interesting thing. It involves a "letting go." If I trust you with something, it means I give it to you. It passes from my hand to yours. It is no longer in my possession. If I have confidence in your character and abilities, there is *relief* at the passing. I no longer worry or concern myself with the matter. It is, as they say, "in good hands." This means that trust is very much about the person being trusted. It also means acceptance. If I trust you, then I accept what you say and what you do.

Corrie once reflected on an event that took place when she was no more than ten or eleven as she traveled with her father on the train from Amsterdam to Haarlem. She had stumbled upon a poem that had the word *sexsin* among its lines.

> And so, seated next to Father in the train compartment, I suddenly asked, "Father, what is sexsin?"
>
> He turned to look at me, as he always did when answering a question, but to my surprise he said nothing. At last he stood up, lifted his traveling case from the rack over our heads, and set it on the floor.
>
> "Will you carry it off the train, Corrie?" he said.
>
> I stood up and tugged at it. It was crammed with the watches and spare parts he had purchased that morning.
>
> "It's too heavy," I said.
>
> "Yes," he said. "And it would be a pretty poor father who would ask his little girl to carry such a load. It's the same way, Corrie, with knowledge. Some knowledge is too heavy for children. When you are older and stronger you can bear it. For now you must trust me to carry it for you."
>
> And I was satisfied. More than satisfied—wonderfully at peace. There were answers to this and all my hard questions—for now I was content to leave them in my father's keeping.

We are called to trust God in the same way. Including the ultimate area of trust: his will.

## The Two Wills of God

When it comes to the will of God, the first thing the Bible teaches is intriguing. There isn't *one* will of God. There's *two*.

The first will of God is his sovereign will, his overarching will. If I were across from you, I would grab a napkin and draw a big circle for this. Ridiculous, I know, for something like that to picture God's will. Wrong, in fact. It implies there is something outside of the circle, and there isn't. But let's not get so theologically sophisticated that we can't use a circle to make a point.

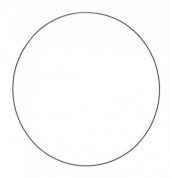

Nothing falls outside of this sense of the will of God. He is the Ruler and Creator of the universe. Nothing happens that he doesn't want to happen, and what he wants to happen will. Look at how this is talked about in the Bible: "All the people of the earth are nothing compared to him. He has the power to do as he pleases among the angels of heaven and with those who live on earth. No one can stop him or challenge him, saying, 'What do you mean by doing these things?'" (Daniel 4:35 NLT 1996). Does this mean that God then wills people to sin, or that he violates the free will of human beings? No. Which brings us to the *second* will of God. The

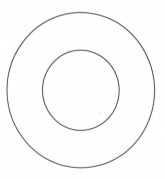

second will of God is what might be called God's "wishes." This has to do with God's desires, the choices he hopes we will make that please him. Some call it his *permissive* will.

Time for another circle. This one is drawn inside the first circle.

God doesn't force his permissive will on us; he only calls us to it.

Whenever the New Testament makes mention of our responsibility in light of God's will, the Greek word used for "will" is always *thelema*, which does not speak to God's resolute intention. Instead, it is a word that expresses his wish or desire—a wish or desire that demands our cooperation for its fulfillment. For example, we read these words from the New Testament: "God wants you to be holy and stay away from sexual sins. He wants each of you to learn to control your own body. Don't use your body for sexual sin like the people who do not know God" (1 Thessalonians 4:3-5 NCV). We know that not everyone honors God in this way; he *wants* us to, but permits us to choose. Within God's permissive will, there is enormous freedom—even the freedom to go against what he wishes. We can choose to sin, to rebel, to go our own way. Or we can choose to follow him.

That is what was at hand with the Tree of Life in the Garden of Eden. God had created a paradise for Adam and Eve, and said, "It's all yours. The beauty, the pleasure, the wonderment of all that I've created. So run free, play, enjoy, create, eat from any tree, drink from any stream." But then God said: "But you must not eat from the tree of the knowledge of good and evil, for when you eat of it you will surely die" (Genesis 2:17). God created an opportunity—a choice—to make sure that it was a relationship, that it truly was a decision that Adam and Eve would make to be related to him. The knowledge of good and evil means the decision to determine what is good and what is evil for yourself—leaving God's will and following your own.

And Adam and Eve chose.

Living within the permissive will of God is still our struggle. So let's explore this aspect of God's will a bit more.

## THE DRAMA OF TRUST

The primary will of God for your life is the same as it is for everybody else—to know and to love God. When someone asked Jesus what the heart of life was all about, what the ultimate law to follow was, this is what he said: 'You must love the LORD your God with all your heart, all your soul, and all your mind.' This is the first and greatest commandment" (Matthew 22:37-38 NLT). We came into that love relationship through our acceptance of Christ's work on the cross.

The second major dimension of God's will for your life is his moral will. God's moral will has to do with how we should think and believe, what we should value and honor, and from that, how we should live. As Paul wrote to the church at Colossae, "We have not stopped praying for you and asking God to fill you with the knowledge of his will through all spiritual wisdom and understanding" (Colossians 1:9). Paul would also write,

> Do not conform any longer to the pattern of this world, but be transformed by the renewing of your mind. Then you will be able to test and approve what God's will is—his good, pleasing and perfect will. (Romans 12:2)

Here is where we need to spend some time. We want to trust God, and specifically by following his will for our lives. But that means following his moral will, for it is precisely his moral will that is at the heart of trust—for it is the moral will of God that is our primary compass. So many times we skip right past God's moral will in trying to figure out what God wants us to do—looking for all kinds of signs, and opening and closing doors—when God's moral will for our life is already speaking to what we should or should not do.

If you want to know what God's moral will is, just ask yourself this question: What does the Bible say? Yes, that seems simplistic. And interpreting the Bible is not always easy. But most of the time, it *is* simple. Notice how the apostle Paul explained it in his second letter to Timothy: "All Scripture is inspired by God and is useful to teach us what is true and to make us realize what is wrong in our lives. It straightens us out and teaches us to do what is right. It is God's way of preparing us in every way, fully equipped for every good thing God wants us to do" (2 Timothy 3:16-17 NLT 1996).

For example, let's say you're struggling with a particular sexual issue, such as having sex outside of marriage. You're wondering whether that's what God would have you to do or not. You desire it, it's appealing to you, but you don't know; you want to know God's will on the matter. So you go to the Bible, and you read this passage in Hebrews: "Honor marriage, and guard the sacredness of sexual intimacy between wife and husband. God draws a firm line against casual and illicit sex" (Hebrews 13:4 *The Message*). Now that's pretty clear, isn't it? So there's your direction. Now I know that one's a slam dunk, but it does show how it works. Through the Bible, God has addressed thousands upon thousands of situations, circumstances, choices and decisions.

But perhaps you don't think the moral will of God applies to much of real life—at least, once you get beyond the Ten Commandments. Let's see. Let's say I'm trying to decide whether or not to take advantage of a particular job opportunity. I begin by making an analysis of the offer in terms of money and benefits, whether the position fits my gifts and abilities, and whether or not I think it's a good company. Let's say all of that looks good. So does God want me to take the job, or not? I'm already tempted to blow off the question, because all the signs look good, and for the life of me, I don't know how God's moral will could have anything to do with this—it's just a job. Right?

But let's dig a little deeper. Let's say I have a wife and young children, and the new job would require an enormous amount of travel that would strain an already fragile marriage, or make me a stranger to my kids during a tenuous time in their life. Or perhaps it would rip my wife and kids out of a context that is integral to their health and wholeness and happiness, such as a school or nearby family. Or maybe the family angle is fine, but the job itself is in a questionable profession, or has ties to some products or companies no follower of Christ should be comfortable with, and my position would directly—or indirectly—make me a supporter if not an advocate. Or let's say that the job would take me out of a particular ministry in a church where God is using me in an instrumental and decisive manner. Suddenly what seemed to be dollars and cents, geography and career track, becomes filled with issues directly related to knowing and following God's moral will for my life.

Here's one of the most important biblical principles you could ever know: God's will for your life is always, first and foremost, a moral will. If you're struggling with whether or not God wants you to do something, or whether or not it's okay with God, and you know it goes against his moral will for your life, you can stop struggling. God has already spoken and made his will known to you,

Figure 8.3: Used by permission of the Corrie ten Boom House Foundation.

because his guidance for the day-in, day-out flow of your life is primarily moral. The question is whether you will trust it.

One night in the Beje, while Holland desperately fought a battle against a German invasion it would eventually lose, dogfights raged overhead, streaking the sky above with fire. Corrie heard her sister stirring in the kitchen, and decided to get up and join her.

Suddenly there was an explosion, rattling the dishes in the cupboard. Corrie and Betsie stayed up another hour, talking. When Corrie returned to her bed, she found a jagged piece of metal, ten inches long, which had cut through her pillow where her head had been laying.

"Betsie, if I hadn't heard you in the kitchen—"

But Betsie put a finger on her mouth. "Don't say it, Corrie! There are no 'ifs' in God's world. And no places that are safer than other places. The center of His will is our only safety—O Corrie, let us pray that we may always know it!"

She was right. The center of God's will, and specifically his moral will, is the safest place on earth.

There's more to digest here. Namely, that in most situations, God's will for your life doesn't go any further than his ultimate will—that you know him and be in a relationship with him—and then his moral will. The Bible gives the impression that once you are in a relationship with God, and stay within his moral will, the rest is up to you. God may not have a particular preference for what you do, or do not, do. God gives you the freedom to choose.

Let's go back to the Garden of Eden. God was very clear to Adam and Eve: "You are free to eat from any tree in the garden; but you must not eat from the tree of the knowledge of good and evil, for when you eat of it you will surely die" (Genesis 2:16-17). That was God's moral will—but also the freedom he gave for choice.

Garry Friesen writes that you can imagine that when Adam got hungry, and turned to Eve, he said, "I think we should eat."

Eve said, "Why don't you go out and get some fruit, and I'll fix it up."

Adam went out, got some fruit, gave it to Eve, and sat back and waited for dinner. But then Eve said, "Adam, which of these fruits do you want me to fix? I want to follow God's will, but I'm not sure what he wants me to do. Would you go ask him what I should do for supper?"

Adam went out to talk to God, but then came back in a few minutes. Eve asked, "What does God want us to do?"

"Well, he didn't really say."

"What do you mean he didn't say?"

"He didn't say! He just repeated what he told us before—that we could eat from any tree of the garden except from the tree of the knowledge of good and evil."

"Did any of this fruit come from there?"

"Nope, not a one."

"So what should I make?"

"Well, let's start off with apples."

So they do—but then Eve said, "How should I fix them? Should I slice them, dice them, mash them, bake them in a pie, make them into a cobbler or just make a fruit salad? I don't want to do anything displeasing to God—be a sweetheart and go back one more time to ask him."

So Adam returns to God, and comes back.

"What did he say?"

"Same thing. From any tree we may eat freely, but from the tree of the knowledge of good and evil, you shall not eat." That's when it clicked with them—that one moral law covered the will of God for their life. As long as they didn't get any fruit from that one tree, they couldn't miss doing what God wanted!

Now let's go back to our job situation. Let's say that under God's moral leadership, you determine that whatever job you take has to honor your basic gifts and passions, protect your family life, keep you in the city you're now in for the sake of a particular ministry investment you're making, and be with a business that has integrity. But once that's covered, there might be hundreds, even thousands of jobs that would make that cut. In other words, it would be a mistake to automatically assume that God has one and *only* one company out there for you for you to join. His will in the matter may not, and probably does not, go past the moral level.

Take marriage as another example. The Bible doesn't say you *have* to get married. Furthermore, nowhere in the Bible does it teach that there is one and *only* one "Mr. Right" or "Miss Right" out there for you. All the Bible talks about are the moral dynamics to whom you *should* marry. So there might be any number of people out there that you could marry that God would be more than willing to bless and make you "one" with.

We all want God's will to be specifically laid out like a map. Go here, do this, take that job, marry that person. Nine times out of ten, what God gives us is more of a compass. So can there a specific will for your life beyond God's moral will? Yes, there *can* be a specific, individual will of God for our life that can come into play. It's just less common; it doesn't present itself on a regular basis. God's will for your life is primarily moral, and that moral will guides the bulk of our day-in, day-out decisions. And within that moral will, there can be equally valid moral choices. Yet there can still be an individual will for your life that reflects God's unique hand of guidance; places he wants you to specifically go, things he wants you to specifically do. Much of this is based on who he has made you to be; your gifts and abilities, your personality and passions. He made you to be a unique individual, and there are unique things he has in mind for each of us.

## CIRCUMSTANCES

We often interpret God's will for us through circumstances. Have you ever prayed, or just thought to yourself, "God, if you want me to take this job, have them call me by ten o'clock this morning"? They call at eleven, but you figure you didn't set your clock exactly right after the time change last weekend, so you count it a "Go" from God.

Or maybe you run into an old high-school acquaintance, by chance, and it's been years since you've seen them or heard from them. And boy, did they clean up over the years. Wouldn't you know, you're both single, and now living in the same city! It must be fate—so you automatically think of romance, even marriage.

Or you're wondering whether or not you should move into a new house, and then the next day, you drive by your dream house—one that you've driven by a hundred times—and wouldn't you know, there's a "For Sale" sign out front. Instant thought? *God must want me to move.*

We've all thought this way, or at least been tempted to. And it can be legitimate. God *can* work through circumstances. He can open and close doors, create opportunities for us, and then place them in our path in order to direct our steps or confirm a particular direction. Consider this account from the book of Acts: "They went to Phrygia, and then on through the region of Galatia. Their plan was to turn west into Asia province, but the Holy Spirit blocked that route. So they went to Mysia and tried to go north to Bithynia, but the Spirit of Jesus wouldn't let them go there either" (Acts 16:6-7 *The Message*). Isn't that interesting? A series of circumstances blocked one way, and then another, pointing them toward where God wanted them to go. We don't know what the circumstances were, but they looked back on them and said, "You know, it was just a God-thing."

Circumstances entice us to move forward, to check something out, to explore something new. When that first, tentative step is met by another encouragement, another open door, another confirmation, we move further and further on. And it can be exhilarating; we look back, and in hindsight, we can see a whole trail of events where God was clearly leading us, step by step. This is why there have been countless times that I have prayed, "God, I've applied everything I know about your moral will to this decision, I've been praying like mad, please, help me to be sensitive to any and all circumstances you might use to direct me."

Or sometimes, it's like this: "God, please, as best as I know, this is the path I am to take. All I know is to start down it. But if it's not, send me a red flag, anything that will help me know that I'm off course. Everything seems to point toward moving ahead, so I am, but if this is something you don't want me to do, please let me know—let doors be closed, prompt those around me to see what I can't see, bring some aspect of this to light that I may not be thinking about."

That kind of prayer is different than setting up some kind of experiment or test for God where he is supposed to jump in a box and perform through circumstances. Such as, "God, if you want me to do this, have the phone ring . . . NOW!" Okay, didn't ring, so I'm off the hook. Or "God, if you want me to take the job, make the next two lights green. No, make that yellow." That's making God a joke, as if he's some kind of leprechaun or genie. That's not what this is about. This is about giving God permission to act, permission to direct your life, asking for his guidance, and then asking for sensitivity to read between the lines. Which is why I'll also pray this: "And God, help me to be discerning about what I see and hear so that I can truly sense your leading."

After the German occupation, the Beje became a place where

Figure 8.4: Used by permission of the Corrie ten Boom House Foundation.

Jews could find safety and comfort. When they began offering the most simple of Christian hospitality to Jewish persons, they had no idea they would find themselves part of the underground network hiding Jews from arrest. But circumstance and opportunity led increasingly toward this very thing. "My job was simply to follow his leading one step at a time," Corrie writes, "holding every decision up to him in prayer. I knew I was not clever or subtle or sophisticated; if the Beje was becoming a meeting place for need and supply, it was through some strategy far higher than mine."

That kind of prayer is important because there are a lot of open doors that God never opened—we did—and there are a lot of coincidences that are just that—coincidences. It's a mistake to think that every need, every opportunity, every circumstance, every event that comes our way is a calling from God, or a direction from God. We need to be very careful about saying what is, or is not, his leading, particularly when we have a very strong desire to go a certain way. Then we'll read anything and everything into the direction we want to go.

And there's always God's moral will to consider. Let me drive that one home a bit. One of the things you'll hear people say is, "But you don't understand—these circumstances are so unique, this situation is so unique, everything came together in such an unbelievable way. . . . I know the Bible says one thing, but let me just walk you through all that's happened!"

Don't fall for it. In fact, let me raise the stakes on this one a bit. Discovering and pursuing God's will isn't just about finding what God wants, and if you don't, your life choices are just kind of neutral, or maybe just not optimal. One of the realities that the Christian faith proclaims is true is that there really is a being called Satan who is alive and well on planet earth, and if you don't think he can orchestrate a few circumstances himself to lead you down the wrong path, you've underestimated him. And that path isn't neutral; it's deadly. So if God's moral will has spoken to your situation, it must take precedent over the circumstances—no matter what they are.

## ACTIVE TRUST

Which brings us back to trust, and how it's not simply about decisions regarding career or marriage, but regarding virtue and value. If the heart of God's will for your life is moral, then the heart of following it is going to be moral in nature.

It was years after her prison experience, at a church service in Munich, that Corrie saw him. He was a balding, heavy-set man in a gray overcoat, but she remembered him in a different guise. He was the former SS man who had stood guard at the shower room door in the processing center at Ravensbrück. She saw him as she had seen him years before: in a blue uniform and visored cap with a skull and crossbones, and with leather riding crop. She had been forced to walk naked past this leering, laughing, cruel man. Throughout the passing of the years, this was the first actual jailer that she had seen since her release. Suddenly it all returned. The roomful of mocking men, the heaps of clothing, her sister's pain-blanched face.

He came to her immediately. "How grateful I am for your message, *Fraulein*," he said. "To think that, as you say, he has washed my sins away!" Then he thrust out his hand to shake hers, and told her what she already knew. "I was a guard at Ravensbrück. I have become a Christian. I know that God has forgiven me for the cruel things that I did there, but I would like to hear it from your lips as well. *Fraulein*, will you forgive me?"

Corrie thought to herself that she could not. Her sister had died in there. It was too much to erase, too much to forgive, too much to ask. She who had spoken so often to so many about the need to forgive kept her hand at her side.

Undaunted, his hand remained outstretched.

She just looked at it.

Yet she knew that forgiveness was not an act of emotion, but an act of the will. It was a decision. One that would echo throughout her life. Suddenly she thought to herself, "Jesus died for this man; am I going to ask for more?" So she prayed, "Lord Jesus, forgive me and help me to forgive him." She tried to smile, she struggled to raise her hand, but could not. She felt nothing, not even the slightest spark of warmth or charity.

Again she prayed. "Lord Jesus, I cannot forgive him. Give me your forgiveness."

Then she took his hand—and when she did, the most extraordinary thing happened. From her shoulder along her arm and through her hand a current seemed to pass from her to him, while into her heart sprang a love for this stranger that almost overwhelmed her.

To me, this is the heart of finding and following God's will, being rooted in his moral will.

## A Gift

One of the great gifts I received was time alone in the Beje. When

I arrived, I was the only "guest." I was told to make myself at home, and to feel free to wander throughout the house. I opened the door to the alley and thought of the comings and goings of those who had lived there. I went up the winding staircase to Corrie's room and entered the hiding place where so many had been hidden and had their lives spared as a result. I wandered back down to the reception room, all looking as if the Ten Booms had just gone out but would return any moment. Even the watch shop was still open for business; a small grandfather clock resides in our living room from its shelves to this day.

I found myself returning to the dining room just up from the main floor, and directly off the alleyway entrance. The warmth of love that must have permeated the Beje seemed still present. The Dutch have a word that describes a home, a family, a feeling. *Gezellig.* It means pleasant, cozy, entertaining. Gezellig applies to a family that plays together, lives in harmony and joy. It's what Corrie described in later years as the "art of living." And that is what trust is. An art of living.

In that room my eyes drifted to an embroidery of a crown. I knew instantly what it was. Corrie would often hold up the piece of cloth, first showing the beauty of the embroidered side, with all the threads forming a beautiful picture. This, she would say, is God's plan for our lives. Then she would flip it over to show the tangled, confused underside, illustrating how we view our lives from a human standpoint.

A poem would then be recited, a rendition from Grant Colfax Tullar:

My life is but a weaving between my God and me
I do not choose the colors, He worketh steadily.
Oftimes He weaveth sorrow, and I in foolish pride,
Forget He sees the upper, and I the underside.

Not till the loom is silent and the shuttles cease to fly.
Will God unroll the canvas and explain the reason why,
The dark threads are as needful in the skillful Weaver's hand,
As the threads of gold and silver in the pattern He has planned.

# 9

## DACHAU CONCENTRATION CAMP
## DACHAU, GERMANY

### YOU WILL HAVE DOUBTS

*If you don't have any doubts*
*you are either kidding yourself or asleep.*

FREDERICK BUECHNER

✦ ✦ ✦

Figure 9.1: Martin St-Amant/Wikimedia Commons

"Keep quiet or you'll end up in Dachau."

The phrase quickly entered the common parlance. Its dreaded name soon became a byword for unspeakable horror which was known to take place within its walls.

Located just outside of Munich, Germany, the Dachau Concentration Camp is one of the most chilling places I have ever visited. It opened on March 22, 1933, the first of the German concentration camps and the only one open throughout the entire Nazi era. It became a model for every other concentration camp, an "academy of terror," spawning camps with names such as Auschwitz, Buchenwald, Bergen-Belsen and Ravensbrück. Dachau did not close until liberated by American troops on April 29, 1945. But not before over 200,000 human beings from across Europe were robbed of their freedom, tortured and exploited, and—for tens of thousands—eventually killed.

I don't know why I always wanted to visit a concentration camp, but I always did. Perhaps I wanted to get some sense of how such a thing could have happened; or perhaps empathetically share in the greatest atrocity committed by humans against humans in modern history. I'm not sure. But I was compelled to set foot on at least one of those blood-saturated compounds, and eventually I did.

The experience begins with one of the most infamous phrases in modern history. Woven into the steel of the front entrance is the German phrase that was put on the entrance of every concentration camp: "*Arbeit macht frei.*" "Work makes you free."

The door swings open to guard towers and a barbed-wire perimeter encompassing a vast area where prisoners would gather for roll call. Here were the individual barracks—each designed for forty men, but up to four hundred would be forced inside each one. Some were set aside for medical experiments that almost defy description in terms of horror. In fact, the first use of concentration camp inmates for medical experimentation was at Dachau. Early experiments focused on the human body's reactions to rapid decompressions and lack of oxygen at high altitudes, conducted in a mobile decompression chamber. This soon descended into "terminal experiments," in which the subject's death was planned from the start, to see how long someone could stay alive when the air supply was gradually thinned out. This soon led to the establishment of an Institute for Applied Research in Defense Science for the express purpose of carrying out medical research in the concentration camps. From simulated parachute jumps to immersion in icy water, the injection of pus to the insertion of gangrenous tissue, horror reigned.

Figure 9.2: Dorsm365/Wikimedia Commons

Walking toward the back of the camp, then turning to the left, are the gas chambers, disguised as showers, built toward the end of the war to speed up the execution of the prisoners. It's numbing to see even today. But nothing can mirror what the liberators themselves experienced. Bodies piled upon bodies, broken, emaciated corpses that portrayed the horror they had endured.

As you journey beyond the chambers, you find the site where the prisoners would be shot at point-blank range. I wasn't sure at first what I was seeing; there was a shallow ditch for what seemed to be a dried-up stream. Then I stumbled on the plaque which said the ditch was dug to carry away the river of blood from execution after execution.

It was too much for the ground to soak.

It's difficult to describe a visit to Dachau. Yes, there are buildings and reconstructions. Historical markers abound, helping you grasp the significance of your surroundings. But there's more. When you walk into Dachau, you walk into a mausoleum of human pain and suffering. No one laughs or talks above a whisper, even in the open air of the barracks or assembly grounds. There is a blanket of sobriety, a weight of gravitas. It is as if you are on holy ground. How ironic that space drenched with such a sense of the sacred is the seed of so much spiritual doubt. While many found faith of its deepest and most vibrant nature on the grounds of Dachau, others lost it forevermore.

Holocaust survivor Elie Wiesel put the memory of the horrors of his experience to words in a book that was appropriately called *Night*. One of the nightmares he describes has to do with the hanging of a young boy who was suspected of sabotage in a Nazi death camp by the German Gestapo.

They began by torturing the boy. When he would not confess, they sentenced him to death with two other prisoners, leading all three in chains to the gallows. It was to be a public execution, and thousands of prisoners were forced to watch. While the head of the camp read the verdict, all eyes were on the child. His face was pale, and he was nervously biting his lips. No more than twelve years old, Wiesel writes that he had the face of a sad angel. The three victims mounted the chairs, and their necks were placed within the nooses.

The child said nothing.

Suddenly, someone cried out, "Where is God? Where is he?"

No one answered.

The executioner then tipped the three chairs over so that the bodies fell, jerking to a stop at the end of the ropes. Though the crowd was large, not a sound was heard. The only movement was the setting of the sun on the horizon. The only noise was the sound of men weeping.

The two adults died instantly. Their tongues hung swollen, tinged with blue. But the third rope, the one holding the little boy, was still moving. For more than half an hour, he hung there, struggling between life and death, dying in slow agony under their eyes. Unfeeling and insolent, the guards ordered the prisoners to march past the two dead bodies, along with the still struggling boy.

As Wiesel passed, he writes that he could not help but turn and gaze into the boy's eyes. As he did, behind him, he heard the voice say again, "Where is God now?" And Wiesel said that the inner voice of his heart answered, "Where is He? Here He is—He is hanging here on this gallows." For Elie Wiesel, that ended any chance of him relating to God. For him, God died that day.

But God didn't "die" for everyone. I read an interview of a man by the name of Christian Reger who spent four years as a prisoner at Dachau for nothing more than belonging to the Confessing Church, the branch of the German state church which opposed Hitler. Later he became a leader of the International Dachau Committee, and returned to the grounds in order to restore the camp as a monument so that the world would not forget. In the interview, Reger reflected how the German philosopher Nietzsche said a man can undergo torture if he knows the *why* of his life. "But I, here at Dachau, learned something far greater. I learned to know the Who of my life. He was enough to sustain me then, and is enough to sustain me still."

Are you there yet? In the face of staggering questions and assaults against your faith, and even against God's character, are you content with the *Who* of your life as opposed to the often-empty nature of the *why?*

Throughout our faith journey we will experience doubt—doubt about the goodness of God, the wisdom of God, even the truth of God. Dachau moments. Moments when you wonder what God is *really* like. Sometimes it can seem that the God of the Bible acts in ways that we would never dream of acting, which makes it hard to believe *that* God—or what we think we *know* about that God—is *right,* much less that he is worthy of worship and obedience.

Listen to the words of this blog post titled "If I Was God":

If I was god, the following words and phrases would not exist . . .

War, Hunger, Drugs, Murder, Disease, Poverty, Rape, Poor, Fight, Genocide, Famine, Jealousy, Slavery, Homeless, Conflict, Hate, Natural Disaster, Greed, Crime, Oppression, Victim, Gun, Third World, Accident, Weapon, Atrocity, Bomb, Abortion, Molestation, Dictator, Steal, Mental Illness, Sorrow, Kill, Sadness, Loneliness, Death, Anger, Apology, Old, Need, Evil, Sick, Cancer, Hell . . .

If I was god, human beings wouldn't have a need for anything. There would be no hunger or poverty. There would be plenty of everything to go around for everybody . . .

If I was god, natural disasters would not occur. The universe would be a beautifully calm place. Earth would be free from earthquakes, tsunamis, volcanic eruptions and any other "natural" occurrence that has a chance to kill humans.

If I was god . . . things would be a lot different.

Strike a chord? It does with a lot of people. For what it's worth, such moments are normal. They are simply moments of questions, of doubt, of facing the mystery of God in light of the reality of our broken world. It's what you *do* with them that matters.

Of course, much that we lay at God's feet belongs at our own. Much of the evil and suffering and insanity of this world is self-inflicted. Dachau itself was a reflection of human depravity, and was meant to be as evil as it was. Even the first camp commandant, an SS officer named Theodor Eicke, had been plucked from a psychiatric hospital due to his sanity being questioned by the local Nazi leadership. Fitting, in a way, as Dachau was insanity made manifest.

But it was human insanity, not God's.

When Susan (my wife) and I went to Dachau, we took a taxi from our hotel in Munich. We told the driver where we wanted to go. He didn't say anything for a long time. He just drove. Then, out of the blue, he said in a thick German accent, "Where you go, it is a very painful place." Then he paused again,

Figure 9.3: Kwz/Wikimedia Commons

and said, "When I was ten or eleven years old, my teacher took us here. She said, 'We were responsible for two world wars—now we are responsible for freedom.'" Then he paused again, and said, "Those were the right words to say, I think."

I think so too.

## God and Questions

But there still remain questions. Not simply over the dysfunction of the world, but raw intellectual hurdles that we don't know how to leap.

Author Dan Brown wrote the bestselling novel *The Da Vinci Code*. At first glance, the plot isn't anything that stands out above the normal mystery fare: The murder of a curator at the Louvre in

Paris leads to a trail of clues found in the work of Leonardo da Vinci and to the discovery of a centuries old secret society. But as the plot unfolds, we find woven throughout the narrative a thoroughgoing rejection of the truth of the Christian faith. Specifically, Brown suggests that the church invented the deity of Jesus. So it wasn't just a novel. Brown put forward a blend of fiction and historical assertion that suggests that the entire foundation upon which Christianity is established is false.

In an interview to promote a later book, he was asked, "Are you religious?" Here was his answer:

> I was raised Episcopalian, and I was very religious as a kid. Then, in eighth or ninth grade, I studied astronomy, cosmology, and the origins of the universe. I remember saying to a minister, "I don't get it. I read a book that said there was an explosion known as the Big Bang, but here it says God created heaven and Earth and the animals in seven days. Which is right?" Unfortunately, the response I got was, "Nice boys don't ask that question." A light went off, and I said, "The Bible doesn't make sense. Science makes much more sense to me." And I just gravitated away from religion.

I had a very different experience with questions when I was young. At the ripe old age of nine, it dawned on me that the reason I was a Christian was because my parents were Christians. Or at least, they held a Christian worldview and disposition. Like a thunderbolt from the blue, it hit me: *That's why I believed it all; I had been raised to!* Which, of course, did not make it true.

My preadolescent brain quickly surmised that if I had been born in India, I would have been raised a Hindu. It would have been *Hinduism* that I would have believed and accepted. If I had been born in Iran, my parents would have raised me to accept the *Muslim* faith. I remember panicking—what if I wasn't born in the right country! My entire eternity suddenly seemed to rest on whether my family of origin was geographically correct.

I went to my mother, who was innocently working in the kitchen and unaware of my spiritual crisis, and asked, "Mom, why are we Christians? You did check it out first, didn't you? How do you and Dad know we're believing the right one?"

I remember her rising from her work, and looking at me for what seemed an eternity. Then she seemed to decide how to respond. She did not dismiss me, or give me a quick "Don't worry" kind of reply that would have trivialized my question. She knew me well enough to know that I was serious about the question, and that how she answered me could prove to be decisive to my spiritual future. She also resonated with the question, for though I did not know it at the time, she had yet to fully embrace the Christian faith herself. So she said something that was very unusual for a parent to say to her nine-year-old son.

"Jim, your father and I have looked at all of the faiths of the world, and have determined that Christianity is the right religion. But you have to come to that in your own mind. So you are welcome to look into all of the world's religions, and come to your own conclusions. And if, at the end, you want to go to a different church, or believe something else, you may."

Inwardly I heaved a huge sigh of relief. Not just because they had apparently done their homework (I had not given them credit for being as reflective about the matter as I had been), but also because I was allowed to pursue my questions without fear of retribution. There was something comforting, even reassuring, about such freedom. I was taught that doubt, by itself, was not wrong; it was simply the fuel that energizes faith to seek understanding.

## REAPPRAISING THE GREAT DOUBTER

The truth is that the God of the Bible invites us to bring our questions to him for answers—or at least for trust. For that, we need look no further than the most famous questioner in the entire Bible. Someone who asked so many questions of Jesus—and about Jesus—that we have given him the surname "doubting." Yes, as in "Doubting Thomas."

The first time we meet Thomas in the Bible is at the very beginning of Jesus' ministry as he was pulling together the men and women who would form his inner circle of followers:

> One of those days Jesus went out to a mountainside to pray, and spent the night praying to God. When morning came, he called his disciples to him and chose twelve of them, whom he also designated apostles: Simon (whom he named Peter), his brother Andrew, James, John, Philip, Bartholomew, Matthew, Thomas, James son of Alphaeus, Simon who was called the Zealot, Judas son of James, and Judas Iscariot, who became a traitor. (Luke 6:12-16)

Reflect on the list; Jesus gathered together an interesting group. If you know their backstories, you know that they were earthy day laborers, disreputable financial players, and one certified two-faced scoundrel whose name would forever become associated with betrayal. Also in that mix was a spiritual seeker named Thomas who had a lot of questions. You can only imagine that he had been firing them off to Jesus long before Jesus picked him to be part of his core group to invest in. So think about that. A seeker, a doubter, an invited "disciple" who wasn't yet sure about the whole thing. And that was okay.

Now let's fast forward. Jesus had been making waves left and right with his ministry and miracles, talks and teachings. The religious establishment became threatened—so much so that when he was in Judea, they tried to kill him. Jesus then moved on to another city. Then he heard that his close friend, Lazarus, had

Figure 9.4: Odcdtd45/Wikimedia Commons

become dangerously ill. Lazarus's sisters, Mary and Martha, asked Jesus to come. But Lazarus lived in Judea.

Jesus never hesitated.

Neither did someone else:

> [Then Jesus] said to his disciples, "Let's go to Judea again."
>
> But his disciples objected. "Teacher," they said, "only a few days ago the Jewish leaders in Judea were trying to kill you. Are you going there again?" . . .
>
> "Come, let's go see him."
>
> Thomas . . . said to his fellow disciples, "Let's go, too— and die with Jesus." (John 11:7-8, 15-16 NLT)

Is that the Thomas you thought you knew? Someone ready to *die* with Jesus? Even racing ahead of the other disciples in terms of commitment? Probably not.

But that gives us something else to think about. Namely, that there isn't a disconnect between asking *questions* and having *faith*. You see, doubt is about being "in two minds." As Os Guinness has written, doubt is far from unbelief, and even for the believer, nothing to be ashamed of. "To believe," writes Guinness, "is to be 'in one mind' about accepting something as true; to disbelieve is to be 'in one mind' about rejecting it. To doubt is to waver between the two, to believe and disbelieve at once and so to be 'in two minds.'"

And we all have two minds. Frederick Buechner once noted that if you don't have any doubts, "you are either kidding yourself or asleep." Doubt is a *part* of the faith journey, and the Bible records that journey for us in Thomas.

Let me take you to another scene from his life.

Thomas asked Jesus *the* big question. The one every spiritual seeker wants an answer to more than anything else. Here's what he asked: "Thomas said to [Jesus], 'Lord . . . how can we know the way?'" (John 14:5). Isn't that the big one? How can we know what is true? How can we know what to believe? How can we know which way is the right way?

How did Jesus respond?

> Thomas said to [Jesus], "Lord . . . how can we know the way?"
>
> Jesus answered, "I am the way and the truth and the life. No one comes to the Father except through me. If you really knew me, you would know my Father as well. From now on, you do know him and have seen him. . . . Anyone who has seen me has seen the Father." (John 14:5-7, 9)

Now that's arresting. Not just that Thomas asked the question. Not just that Jesus didn't mind him asking the question. *But that he got an answer.*

"Thomas, you want answers to all your questions. Fair enough. I'll give you the answer to all your questions. I am the way. Yes, *the* way. Not 'a' way, but *the* way. You want to connect with God, well, here I am. If you've seen me, you've seen God. Because that's who I am, God in human form, come to earth to show the way. My life is the answer to your questions. My teaching is the answer to your questions; *I* am the answer to your questions."

I've often heard people say, "If God loves us so much, why doesn't he just make it all clear? Why doesn't he just come down and reveal himself?"

He did.

Was that enough for Thomas?

No.

There was one more interaction with Jesus the Bible gives us. The most famous one of all. Jesus had been betrayed, arrested, sentenced and crucified in a single whirlwind span of twenty-four hours. It left Thomas, along with every other disciple, devastated, terrified and confused. Even though Jesus had told them, time and again, that he had come to give his life away, that he was going to lay down his life for the sins of the world, that he would come back from the dead, they still didn't get it. So when he *was* crucified, the wheels of their life came off. And maybe Thomas's wheels most of all. It was as if everything he was starting to believe, starting to trust, was ripped out from underneath him.

So what happened next should come as no surprise. The Bible tells us that three days after his crucifixion, Jesus presented himself to some of the disciples resurrected from the dead. Thomas wasn't there, but he was one of the first ones told about it, and Thomas would have none of it:

> Now Thomas . . . was not with the disciples when Jesus came. So the other disciples told him, "We have seen the Lord!"
>
> But he said to them, "Unless I see the nail marks in his hands and put my finger where the nails were, and put my

hand into his side, I will not believe it." (John 20:24-25)

What did Thomas say? The paraphrase is easy: "I have one more question. And it's one I don't think will ever be answered. And here's my question: Is there *proof?* I know what Jesus said to us. I know what he taught us. I know what I saw him do while he was living. But if he's really who he said he was, if all of that is for real, and he's really come back from the dead, then I need to see it. That's my last question.

*"Where is he?"*

Was that going too far? Was that asking too much?

Apparently not.

A week later his disciples were in the house again, and Thomas was with them. Though the doors were locked, Jesus came and stood among them and said, "Peace be with you!" Then he said to Thomas, "Put your finger here; see my hands. Reach out your hand and put it into my side. Stop doubting and believe."

Thomas said to him, "My Lord and my God!" (John 20:26-28)

This is interesting. A dead man, now alive, turns immediately to one person—Thomas. Why? To let him know that every word, every thought, had been *heard.* His questions had been duly noted.

And here was the answer.

When you look at the life of Jesus, he met every person where they were, and spoke to their deepest needs. Even after the resurrection, his interactions were tailor-made for where they were at.

The Gospel of John was, I believe, inspired for this. John was the last of the four Gospels, and there is every indication he knew very well what Matthew, Mark and Luke had written. He wanted to tell the untold story, which is why 90 percent of what John records is not found in any other Gospel. This includes what happened after the resurrection.

Jesus went to a grieving woman named Mary and comforted her. He went to a guilt-ridden betrayer named Peter, and restored him.

And he went to a man with questions named Thomas, and answered them.

And again, in the most powerful, all-encompassing way imaginable.

Himself.

Will you welcome another paraphrase? "Thomas, I am still the way, the truth, and, as you can see, the life. So put your finger where the nails were driven; Put your hand in my side where the spear was thrust. Is this enough of an answer for you?"

And that is how Thomas came to say, "You are my Lord, and you are my God."

I know what you might be thinking, "Yeah, if Jesus showed up for *me* from the dead, I think I'd say 'My Lord and my God,' too!" Jesus knew you'd think that, because that wasn't the end of the conversation. Jesus had a final word for Thomas that was really more of a word for us: "Because you have seen me, you have believed; blessed are those who have not seen and yet have believed" (John 20:29). Jesus pronounced a blessing on all who would believe without seeing what Thomas saw, without experiencing what Thomas experienced, a blessing on all who would read the record of what happened,

. . . and believe.

All who would like the incredible amount of evidence surrounding the life of Jesus,

. . . and believe.

All who would look to an empty tomb,

. . . and believe.

What Jesus was saying to Thomas was this: "Stop being faith-
less; become a believer. It's not that you can't ask questions; it's not
that there aren't answers. It's about whether you will hide behind
questions, pretend like there are no answers, and then never commit. Faith is not about the end of all questions. It's about reaching
a settled conviction. It's holding the Father's hand and trusting
him to lead us in the journey of life, no matter where he takes us.
It's saying, 'I do not understand it all, or have all the answers, but
I have trust in the One who does.'"

So let's review.

Is the God of the Bible open to our questions?

Yes.

Is he willing to give us answers?

Yes.

Do we get all of our questions answered?

No.

If we understood everything about God, then God would be no
larger than our intellect. I'm sorry, but that's a very small God.
There will always be mystery. The real question is whether there
are *enough* answers. That's the real issue, isn't it? We want to be
sure, beyond any doubt, of what is true and best. The dilemma,
however, is that our spiritual search is for God, and the depth of
God can never be fully explored, much less understood. We will
*always* have unanswered questions, because our subject is God!
Thus the goal of any spiritual search is not to find *every* answer,
but *enough* answers. Everybody lives by faith. The question is what
you are putting your faith in.

Here's what I believe. God is big enough for your questions.
Bring them to him. He's not going to be offended, and it doesn't
invalidate your faith. If it's true (if he's true), then your faith will
stand up to any amount of intellectual scrutiny. I once read that
God is the friend of the honest doubter who dares to talk to God

rather than about him. Let God be that friend.

## And Then They Came for Me

Dachau was designed to be physically tough and psychologically destructive. Inmates were supposed to have a hard wooden bunk and poor food rations; their work was designed to be punitive and degrading. Guards were trained in a wide range of torturous penalties. A favorite was the *Pfahlbaum* torture. Prisoners would be suspended with their arms above and behind them on a long pole. Hung for hours, shoulders would soon dislocate; days produced a slow death.

One of the more famous prisoners subjected to such treatment, sent by Hitler himself, was a Lutheran pastor named Martin Niemoller. He experienced the horror of imprisonment for eight years, being moved finally to Dachau in 1941. According to the memoir of a fellow inmate, Niemoller experienced the regular beatings and degradation of any other prisoner, recalling that the guards made Niemoller

> hop on one foot between them, sometimes crouch and hop. They beat him at the same time to make him more agile. One day he evidently used the name of God (though I could not catch it), for I heard one of the guards shout, "The *Schweinhund* is calling his *Drecksgott* (dirty god). I would like to see if he will help him out of here." Sometimes the Commandant or other officers would stop to watch the play. Then the guards would outdo themselves as they received approving laughs.

Niemoller had been a U-boat captain during World War I, receiving the Iron Cross for his bravery. Early on, he had welcomed the rise of the Nazi party, thinking they would restore Germany's dignity, diminish the communists and instill a sense of moral order. Niemoller met with Hitler privately in 1932, receiving Hitler's assurance that churches would remain free and no pogroms would be instituted against the Jews. Satisfied with his meeting, Niemoller looked forward to the national religious revival that would sweep his homeland—a revival for which he had long prayed.

He soon learned of Hitler's true character and intent, and became one of the most outspoken critics and leaders of the resistance. Along with a young pastor by the name of Dietrich Bonhoeffer and the famed theologian Karl Barth, he became one of the founders of the Confessing Church which arose in protest of Hitler's attempt to control the German Protestant church and to the Nazi state itself.

He was rewarded with Dachau.

This is the great crucible of doubt, and particularly doubt raised by places like Dachau. "Suffering is the most acute trial that faith can face, and the questions it raises are the sharpest, the most insistent and the most damaging that faith will meet." But if met, they are also the most deeply forming.

Dachau did not simply raise questions for Niemoller, it brought the purifying fires that only come when such doubt is faced. It brought Niemoller to a new perspective on his life and commitments, convictions and values. Looking back on his arrest and imprisonment later in life, Niemoller came to regret the early compromises he had made with the Nazis, and blamed himself for pursuing his narrow religious interests:

> First they took the Communists, but I was not a Communist, so I said nothing. Then they took the Social Democrats, but I was not a Social Democrat, so I did nothing. Then it was the trade unionists' turns, but I was not a trade unionist. And then they took the Jews, but I was not a Jew, so I did little. Then when they came and took me, there was no one left who could have stood up for me.

But Dachau did even more for Niemoller. It gave him the opportunity to flesh out his relationship with Christ. Niemoller became not only a pastor to the prisoners, but a leader. As historian Richard Evans writes, "In view of his patient suffering of such maltreatment, and his constantly reiterated faith in God, he gained a considerable degree of moral authority over the other inmates, all of whom he treated undifferentiatingly as victims of an evil regime."

We will all have our Dachau moments. Perhaps not of the same intensity as Niemoller, but they will be intensely real for us. We will either cling to our faith, or abandon it. Cling to it; but know that in order to do so, the doubts that brought us to our crisis must not be ignored.

They must be embraced.

# AFTERWORD

THERE ARE SO MANY MORE PLACES I would like to introduce you
to. The historian David McCullough, in an address to the graduat-
ing Middlebury class of 1986, told them to "go far." He then out-
lined the places he hoped that they would see, from Florence to
Edinburgh, Palenque to Monticello. That is my wish for you as
well. Perhaps we'll have another chance to do it together.

But I hope you have gained the heart of my efforts . . .

With conversion, that it be complete. Christ as Savior and
Lord.

With spirituality, that you would attain a discipline of personal
responsibility to draw near to God and experience the wonders of
intimacy with him.

With hearing God, that you would live a life in willing submission to his voice.

With community, that you would resolve to love others. Nothing more, but nothing less.

With sexuality, that you would be holy.

With calling, that you chase relentlessly after who God made
you to be—and then fulfill that dream.

With the vision of making history, that you would never release
yourself from the passion to make an impact.

With trust, that you would know that you can rely on God's

character and goodness. Really.

And with doubt, that you would know that God is big enough for any question.

I wish these things for you, and I wish them for me. This life is but shadows, Lewis once wrote—real living has yet to begin. But in these shadows, the life to come is forged.

Yes, much of your thinking is about this life—making it all it can be, and should be. All well and good. But as we all age—something I very much feel these days—you begin to see that this life is little more than a warmup for the life to come. A test, if you will, for when and where and how you will be placed. If I have a final word for you, it would be to live the secret Jesus lived—which was living with eternity always in view. This life, in truth, is nothing—except for its chance to be faithful. But what you accomplish in worldly gains?

Meaningless.

I see now with greater clarity than ever that when this life is over, all that will matter is how much of my life I gave over to Jesus, how much I did for him and how much I love him. And, of course, loved others as a result of my love for him.

And that is the most important "place" of all to come to.

# Notes

Chapter 1: The Eagle and Child Pub

page 9    "Lewis struck me as the most": Walter Hooper, in preface to C. S.
          Lewis, *God in the Dock: Essays on Theology and Ethics*, ed. Walter
          Hooper (Grand Rapids: Eerdmans, 1970), p. 12.

page 12   C. S. Lewis recordings: Even a full re-enactment of his famed sermon,
          *The Weight of Glory*, which I heard given by the actor Joss Ackland
          (who played Lewis in the original BBC version of *Shadowlands*, much
          better to my tastes than the Hollywood version with Anthony Hop-
          kins), was difficult listening for most of us present. Translation? *Bor-
          ing*. Much better read than heard.

page 14   the life of C. S. Lewis: There are many biographies available on Lewis,
          including Roger Lancelyn Green and Walter Hooper, *C. S. Lewis: A
          Biography*, rev. ed. (New York: Harvest, 1994); Alan Jacobs, *The Nar-
          nian: The Life and Imagination of C. S. Lewis* (New York: Harper, 2005);
          David C. Downing, *The Most Reluctant Convert: C. S. Lewis's Journey to
          Faith* (Downers Grove, Ill.: InterVarsity Press, 2002); George Sayer,
          *Jack: C. S. Lewis and His Times* (New York: Harper & Row, 1988); Hum-
          phrey Carpenter, *The Inklings* (New York: Ballantine, 1978); and Lew-
          is's own spiritual autobiography, *Surprised by Joy* (New York: Harvest,
          1955).

page 14   "gave in and admitted": Lewis, *Surprised by Joy*, pp. 228-29.

page 15   "the most thoroughly converted man": Walter Hooper, preface, p. 12.

page 16   "Oh, that's easy": C. S. Lewis, in Philip Yancey, *What's So Amazing
          About Grace?* (Grand Rapids: Zondervan, 1997), p. 45.

page 18   "whooshing up": Hubert Dreyfus and Sean Dorrance Kelly, *All Things
          Shining* (New York: Free Press, 2011).

page 18   "of an unsatisfied desire": Lewis, *Surprised by Joy*, p. 17.

page 18   "We are half-hearted creatures": C. S. Lewis, "The Weight of Glory," in
          *The Weight of Glory and Other Essays*, rev. and exp. ed. (New York:
          Macmillan, 1980), pp. 3-4.

| | |
|---|---|
| *page 21* | Francis explicitly mentioned: C. S. Lewis, *Letters to Malcolm* (Orlando, Fla.: Harcourt, 1964), p. 98; C. S. Lewis, "Two Ways with the Self," *God in the Dock: Essays on Theology and Ethics,* ed. Walter Hooper (Grand Rapids: Eerdmans, 1970), p. 193; and *Letters to an American Lady* (Grand Rapids: Eerdmans, 1967), 21 May 1955. |
| *page 23* | "were magnificent, unforgettable": Green and Hooper, *C. S. Lewis: A Biography,* p. 209. |
| *page 23* | "I was . . . writing to expound": C. S. Lewis, *Mere Christianity* (New York: Macmillan, 1952), p. vii. |
| *page 24* | "If the danger in Baxter's time": Jacobs, *The Narnian,* pp. 213-14. |
| *page 25* | conversations with folk who knew Lewis: I caution that these were tales told me while in Oxford by those who claimed to have known and interacted with Lewis. But from all that I know and have read, I would tend to lean on the side of their truth. For example, when the *Daily Telegraph* referred to Lewis as an ascetic, Tolkien wrote to his son, "'Ascetic Mr. Lewis' - !!! I ask you! He put away three pints in a very short session we had this morning, and said he was 'going short for Lent'" (ibid., p. 190). |
| *page 30* | long night talk with Dyson and Tolkien: Adapted from Carpenter, *Inklings,* pp. 45-48, as well as my own journeys to Oxford and dialogues with Oxford folk. |

**Chapter 2: Iona Abbey**

| | |
|---|---|
| *page 31* | "That man is little to be envied": *Iona Abbey and Nunnery,* ed. Christ Tabraham (Edinburgh: Historic Scotland, 2004), p. 1. |
| *page 33* | "the loneliest loneliness in the world": As cited by Deborah and David Douglas, *Pilgrims in the Kingdom: Travels in Christian Britain* (Nashville: Upper Room, 2004), p. 31. |
| *page 33* | "one moment of unblemished glory": Thomas Cahill, *How the Irish Saved Civilization* (New York: Doubleday, 1995), p. 3. |
| *page 34* | witness to the Loch Ness Monster: Adomnan of Iona, *Life of St. Columba,* trans. Richard Sharpe (New York: Penguin, 1995). |
| *page 35* | St. John's cross: Many think that the Celtic Christians were trying to add some deep, mystical meaning to the most famous of Christian symbols through the circle, such as the eternal life found through the cross of Christ, or the perfect unity of the Trinity. In truth, St. John's cross was simply too ambitious. The arms were so long they kept falling off, unable to be supported through the single carving. After numerous repairs, they just added the circle to support the arms. It then spread throughout Scotland and Ireland as a symbol of faith. |
| *page 35* | "thin places": On Celtic beliefs, see Timothy Joyce, *Celtic Christianity: A Sacred Tradition, A Vision of Hope* (Marynoll, N.Y.: Orbis, 1998). |

*page 36*      "Delightful I think it to be in the bosom": As cited by Ted Olsen, *Christianity and the Celts* (Downers Grove, Ill.: InterVarsity Press, 2003), p. 108.

*page 36*      a deep awareness of God's presence: On this see Esther de Waal, *Every Earthly Blessing: Rediscovering the Celtic Tradition* (Harrisburg, Penn.: Morehouse Publishing, 1999), p. xv.

*page 36*      "I will kindle my fire": Alexander Carmichael, "Blessing of the Kindling," in *Carmina Gadelica*, vol. 1, no. 82 (Edinburgh: T. and A. Constables, 1900), p. 231, accessed at <www.sacred-texts.com/neu/celt/cg1/cg1090.htm>.

*pages 36-37*  "The sacred Three": Alexander Carmichael, "Smooring the Fire," in *Carmina Gadelica*, vol. 1, no. 84 (Edinburgh: T. and A. Constables, 1900), p. 235, accessed at <www.sacred-texts.com/neu/celt/cg1/cg1092.htm>.

*page 37*      the world as God's theophany: A "theophany" is a visible appearance or manifestation of God, usually in reference to Old Testament appearances and manifestations. For Eriugena's major work, see *De Natura Divisione*. For a good introduction to his thinking, see John J. O'Mearra, *Eriuguena* (Oxford: Clarendon, 1988).

*page 40*      "inner attentiveness to God": de Waal, *Every Earthly Blessing*, p. 37.

*page 40*      "Christ with me, Christ before me": From Lady Gregory, *Blessed Patrick of the Bells,* book 3 of *A Book of Saints and Wonders* (1906), accessed at <www.sacred-texts.com/neu/celt/saw/saw03.htm>.

*page 41*      St. Columba's Shrine: Certain details and information for various sites described throughout this chapter have been served by Anna Ritchie and Ian Fisher, *Iona Abbey and Nunnery* (Edinburgh: Historic Scotland, 2004).

*page 42*      "Superficiality is the curse": Richard Foster, *The Celebration of Discipline* (San Francisco: Harper & Row, 1978), p. 1.

*page 43*      "a quarter inch long": John O'Donohue, *Anam Cara: A Book of Celtic Wisdom* (New York: HarperCollins, 1997), pp. 89-90.

*page 45*      "Anyone who is not": Dallas Willard, *The Divine Conspiracy* (San Francisco: HarperSanFrancisco, 1998), p. 273.

*page 46*      "law of undulation": I am indebted to C. S. Lewis, particularly *The Screwtape Letters*, for this insight.

*page 48*      "Be thou my vision": On this, see James D. Smith III, "Be Thou My Vision," *Christian History* 60, no. 4 (1998): 37.

*page 48*      "Most of us turned to Christ": Ken Gire, *The Reflective Life* (Colorado Springs: Chariot Victor, 1998), p. 47.

*page 50*      "recreating silences": Thomas Kelly, *A Testament of Devotion* (New York: Harper & Row, 1941), p. 120.

*page 50*      life is meant to be lived: On the two levels of life, see ibid.

*page 50*      "It would revolutionize the lives": As quoted by Gordon MacDonald,

*The Life God Blesses* (Nashville: Thomas Nelson, 1994), p. 71.

*page 50*   from *detachment* to *attachment*: On this, see Foster, *Celebration of Discipline*, p. 15.

*page 50*   "nothing but waiting": Dietrich Bonhoeffer, *Life Together: A Discussion of Christian Fellowship* (New York: Harper & Row, 1954), p. 79.

*page 50*   three primary activities: On this, see Gire, *Reflective Life*, pp. 87-103.

*page 51*   To read the Word: Ibid., p. 89.

*page 51*   "I awake in the name of the Father": Calvin Miller, *The Path of Celtic Prayer: An Ancient Way to Everyday Joy* (Downers Grove, Ill.: InterVarsity Press, 2007), pp. 21, 35.

*page 52*   "Spirit of the living God": *Iona Abbey Worship Book* (Glasgow, Scotland: Wild Goose, 2001), p. 91.

*page 52*   Seven minutes a day with God: On this approach, I am indebted to the little pamphlet *Seven Minutes a Day with God* published by NavPress.

### Chapter 3: St. Catherine's Monastery

*page 55*   "He is there, and He is not silent": Francis A. Schaeffer, *He Is There and He Is Not Silent*, in *The Complete Works of Francis A. Schaeffer*, vol. 1 (Westchester, Ill.: Crossway, 1982), p. 291.

*page 60*   "The man who abides": Owen Chadwick, ed., *Western Asceticism,* The Library of Christian Classics, Ichthus Edition (Philadelphia: Westminster Press, 1958), p. 40.

*page 62*   "How many of you": As cited by M. Blaine Smith, *Knowing God's Will: Finding Guidance for Personal Decisions*, 2nd ed. (Downers Grove, Ill.: InterVarsity Press, 1991), p. 91.

*page 63*   "Go, sit in your cell": Thomas Merton, *The Wisdom of the Desert: Sayings from the Desert Fathers of the Fourth Century* (New York: New Directions, 1960), p. 30.

*page 70*   "This is why I have come": I am not sure from where (or whom) I first began thinking of this scene from the life of Jesus as a model for our time with God, coupled with the impact it can have on our own, but I am relatively confident that it is not wholly original with me.

### Chapter 4: The Apartheid Museum

*page 73*   "Not what a man is": Dietrich Bonhoeffer, *Life Together* (New York: Harper & Row, 1954), p. 25.

*page 75*   the entire museum experience: Throughout this chapter I am indebted to the many printed resources available at the museum, as well the ample material on its website at <www.apartheidmuseum.org>.

*page 77*   "Think of your best moments": Brent Curtis and John Eldredge, *The Sacred Romance: Drawing Closer to the Heart of God* (Nashville: Thomas Nelson, 1997), p. 73.

page 81    "what it means to live communally": Kathleen Norris, *The Cloister Walk* (New York: Riverhead, 1996), p. 21.

page 82    Cornelius Plantinga, *Not the Way It's Supposed to Be: A Breviary of Sin* (Grand Rapids: Eerdmans, 1995), p. 10.

page 83    "No one would be lonely": John Ortberg, *Everybody's Normal Till You Get to Know Them* (Grand Rapids: Zondervan, 2003), pp. 19-20.

page 88    Roger began to change: Adapted from "How God's Children Change," PreachingToday.com, cited from Craig Barnes, author and pastor of National Presbyterian Church, Washington, D.C., in the sermon, "The Blessed Trinity," May 30, 1999.

page 89    "Let me tell you": Ortberg, *Everybody's Normal*, p. 137.

page 90    we need to bring an "emptiness": M. Scott Peck, *The Different Drum: Community Making and Peace* (New York: Touchstone, 1987).

page 93    "Had Nelson Mandela": Adapted from David Aikman, *Great Souls: Six Who Changed the Century* (Nashville: Word, 1998), pp. 61-123.

## Chapter 5: Chartres Cathedral

page 94    "Once upon a time": Colin Ward, *Chartres: The Making of a Miracle* (London: The Folio Society, 1986), p. 5.

page 96    "the whole drama of the redemption": Roland Bainton, *Christianity* (New York: Mariner, 2000), p. 185.

page 96    "We can only imagine": Ward, *Chartres*, pp. 51-52.

page 96    "fulfill an active part": Ibid., p. 53.

page 97    a description of its contents: Ibid., pp. 40-41.

page 97    "To enter Chartres": Michael Wood, Bruce Cole and Adelheid Gealt, *Art of the Western World: From Ancient Greece to Post-Modernism* (New York: Touchstone, 1989), p. 61.

page 99    "Having studied some anatomy": Philip Yancey, *Rumors of Another World* (Grand Rapids: Zondervan, 2003), p. 83.

page 100   "ask themselves whether a building": Owen Chadwick, *A History of Christianity* (New York: Thomas Dunne Books, 1995), p. 143.

page 101   "So, we can [just be] friends": Lauren Winner, *Real Sex: The Naked Truth About Chastity* (Grand Rapids: Brazos, 2005), p. 78.

page 101   nearly three-fourths of all high-school students: See "Nearly 75% of Teens Admit Having Sex," *The Charlotte Observer*, November 25, 1994, p. B1.

page 101   Health records indicate: See "Family Also Influences Boy's Sexuality," *The Charlotte Observer*, November 11, 1993, p. 7A. Also see CDC's *Morbidity and Mortality Weekly Report*, "Vital Signs: Teen Pregnancy— United States, 1991–2009," April 8, 2011 <http://www.cdc.gov/mmwr/preview/mmwrhtml/mm6013a5.htm?s_cid=mm6013a5>.

page 101   households featuring married couples: Sabrina Tavernise, "Married Couples Are No Longer a Majority, Census Finds," *The New York*

*Times*, May 26, 2011 <www.nytimes.com/2011/05/26/us/26marry
.html?src=rechp>.

page 102    In the book *A Return to Modesty*: Wendy Shalit, *A Return to Modesty:
            Discovering the Lost Virtue* (New York: Free Press, 1999).

page 102    "I write for those": Winner, *Real Sex*, p. 22.

page 102    "She is the one who will go home": Stephanie Rosenbloom, "The Tam-
            ing of the Slur," *The New York Times*, July 17, 2006, pp. E1 and E7.

page 104    "The ceremony took place": "Plighting Their Troth—or Whatever,"
            *Breakpoint*, September 21, 2006.

page 108    "Whether Heloise ever came": Ruth A. Tucker, "Heloise and Abelard's
            Tumultuous Affair," *Christian History* 10, no. 2 (1991): 30. I am in-
            debted to Tucker's excellent article throughout this section.

page 108    "left little bits of myself": Bill Hybels and Rob Wilkins, *Tender Love:
            God's Gift of Sexual Intimacy* (Chicago: Moody Press, 1993), p. 38.

page 108    "Don't you know that when you sleep": Winner, *Real Sex*, p. 88.

page 109    A young woman's likelihood of depression: On this see Ross Douthat,
            "Why Monogamy Matters," *The New York Times*, March 6, 2011 <www
            .nytimes.com/2011/03/07/opinion/07douthat.html?partner=rssnyt
            &emc=rss>. On the sociological study, see Mark Regnerus and Jeremy
            Uecker, *Premarital Sex in America* (New York: Oxford University Press,
            2011).

page 109    couples that cohabitate before marriage: Terry Mattingly, Washington
            Bureau religion column, August 21, 2002, cited on PreachingToday
            .com.

page 109    "You can get a large audience together": C. S. Lewis, *Mere Christianity*
            (New York: Macmillan, 1952), p. 75.

page 112    "The *no* to sex outside marriage": Winner, *Real Sex*, p. 38.

page 113    Viking invasion of Chartres: Ward, *Chartres*, p. 6.

page 113    the cathedral was destroyed: Timothy Thibodeau, "Western Christen-
            dom," in *The Oxford History of Christian Worship*, ed. Geoffrey Wain-
            wright and Karen B. Westerfield Tucker (Oxford: Oxford University
            Press, 2004), p. 224.

page 114    "the town's inhabitants": Bainton, *Christianity*, p. 184.

## Chapter 6: The Billy Graham Library

page 115    "That's the first thing": As cited in a display in the Visitor's Center of
            The Cove, the Billy Graham Training Center in Asheville, North Caro-
            lina.

page 117    A recent study found: On the survey by the Pew Forum on Religion
            and Public Life, see <www.christianitytoday.com/ct/2007/november
            /12.18.html>.

page 123    "Doctors practice medicine": Dorothy L. Sayers, "Creed or Chaos?" in
            *The Whimsical Christian* (New York: Macmillan, 1978), p. 50.

*page 124*    "Before I can tell my life": Parker J. Palmer, *Let Your Life Speak: Listening for the Voice of Vocation* (San Francisco: Jossey-Bass, 2000), p. 4.

*page 124*    "I have never had clarity": Brennan Manning, *Ruthless Trust* (New York: HarperCollins, 2000), p. 5.

*page 125*    Thomas Merton, *New Seeds of Contemplation* (New York: New Directions, 1961), p. 29.

*page 125*    "You ask whether your verses": Rainer Maria Rilke, *Letters to a Young Poet*, trans. Stephen Mitchell (New York: Vintage, 1984), pp. 5-6.

*page 126*    "I would like to beg you": Ibid., pp. 34-35.

*page 131*    "Oh God, I cannot prove": Taken from William Martin, *A Prophet with Honor: The Billy Graham Story* (New York: Harper Perennial, 1992), p. 112.

*page 131*    "gave power and authority": From ibid., p. 112.

*page 134*    "Be of good comfort": John Foxe, *Actes and Monuments of These Latter and Perillous Days, Touching Matters of the Church*.

**Chapter 7: Lutherstadt-Wittenberg, Germany**

*page 137*    "Unless I am convicted": On this, see Roland H. Bainton, *Here I Stand: A Life of Martin Luther* (New York: Mentor/Abingdon, 1950), p. 144. See also Bill J. Leonard, *Word of God Across the Ages* (Nashville: Broadman, 1981), p. 34.

*page 137*    "Help, St. Anne": As recorded in his table talk of July 16, 1539, thirty-four years after the event.

*page 137*    Martin Luther was a man of the church: On the life of Luther, see the highly accessible treatment by Bainton in *Here I Stand*. The most complete biography to date, however, is M. Brecht's three-volume work *Martin Luther* (Minneapolis: Fortress).

*page 137*    "By any account, Martin Luther must rank": Graham Tomlin, *Luther and His World* (Downers Grove, Ill.: InterVarsity Press, 2002), p. 6.

*page 138*    The Reformation was more than theological: On this see ibid., p. 71.

*page 138*    "espouse the cause of the faith": Ibid., p. 99.

*page 150*    "vulgarized and commercialized": Martin E. Marty, *A Short History of Christianity*, 2nd ed. (Philadelphia: Fortress, 1987), p. 169.

*page 150*    "When a coin in the coffer rings": Leonard, *Word of God Across the Ages*, p. 38.

*page 150*    "If I profess with the loudest voice": Elizabeth Rundle Charles, *The Chronicles of the Schoenberg Cotta Family* (London, 1864). Commonly misattributed to Luther due to Francis Schaeffer's misattribution of it to him in The Great Evangelical Disaster (Schaeffer attributes it to Luther, but gives no source), it is instead merely inspired by Luther's writings, such as page 81 and following of the third volume of Briefwechsel (correspondence) from *D. Martin Luthers Werke*, the German (Weimar) edition of *Luther's Works*. It is actually written by Charles in her nineteenth-century novel.

*page 151*     The word that was shouted throughout Egypt: On "Enough," I have drawn from the onsite reporting of Erich Bridges with Baptist Press.

*page 152*     "For more than a week": Dwight L. Carlson, "Exposing the Myth that Christians Should Not Have Emotional Problems," *Christianity Today* 42, no. 2 (February 9, 1998): 28.

*page 154*     "He used to say": J. R. R. Tolkien, *The Fellowship of the Ring*, book 1, "Three Is Company."

### Chapter 8: Ten Boom House

*page 155*     "Lord Jesus, I offer myself": Corrie ten Boom, with John and Elizabeth Sherrill, *The Hiding Place* (New York: Bantam, 1971), p. 74.

*page 156*     "a typical tiny old-Haarlam structure": Ibid., p. 2.

*page 157*     "our wise Father in heaven": Ibid., p. 29.

*page 158*     For example, the barracks where she and her sister Betsie: From Luis Palau, *It's a God Thing: Pictures and Portraits of God's Grace* (New York: Doubleday, 2001), p. 158.

*page 158*     "God was good when I was in Ravensbruk": Cited in Billy Graham, *Hope for a Troubled Heart* (Nashville: Thomas Nelson, 1991), p. 39.

*page 159*     "And so, seated next to Father: Ten Boom, *Hiding Place*, pp. 26-27.

*page 160*     use a circle to make a point: Throughout this section, I am indebted to Garry Friesen and J. Robin Maxon, *Decision Making and the Will of God: A Biblical Alternative to the Traditional View* (Portland, Ore.: Multnomah, 1980).

*page 165*     "Betsie, if I hadn't heard you": Ten Boom, *Hiding Place*, p. 67.

*page 165*     Let's go back to the Garden of Eden: Adapted from Friesen and Maxon, *Decision Making*.

*page 170*     "My job was simply to follow": Ten Boom, *Hiding Place,* p. 83.

*page 171*     at a church service in Munich: Adapted from Corrie ten Boom's *Tramp for the Lord* (Old Tappan, N.J.: Fleming H. Revell, 1974), pp. 53-55; also *Hiding Place*, p. 238.

*page 173*     "art of living": Carole C. Carlson, *Corrie ten Boom: Her Life, Her Faith* (Old Tappan, N.J.: Fleming H. Revell, 1983). p. 30.

*page 173*     "My life is but a weaving": Grant Colfax Tullar, quoted in Pam Rosewell Moore, *Life Lessons from the Hiding Place: Discovering the Heart of Corrie ten Boom* (Grand Rapids: Chosen, 2004), pp. 130-31.

### Chapter 9: Dachau Concentration Camp

*page 175*     "If you don't have any doubts": Os Guinness, *In Two Minds: The Dilemma of Doubt and How to Resolve It* (Downers Grove, Ill.: InterVarsity Press, 1976), pp. 24-25.

*page 176*     "Keep quiet or you'll end up": Ian Kershaw, *Hitler—1889-1936: Hubris* (New York: W. W. Norton, 1998), p. 464.

*page 176*     an "academy of terror": Michael Burleigh, *The Third Reich: A New History* (New York: Hill and Wang, 2000), p. 200.

*page 176*     experiments that almost defy description: Richard J. Evans, *The Third Reich at War* (New York: Penguin, 2009), pp. 602-5.

*page 178*     "Where is God now?": Adapted from Elie Wiesel, *Night*, translated from the French by Stella Rodway (New York: Bantam, 1960), pp. 60-62.

*page 179*     "But I, here at Dachau": Philip Yancey, *Where Is God When It Hurts?* (Grand Rapids: Zondervan, 1990), pp. 94-95.

*page 180*     "If I Was God": <www.mwillett.org/atheism/If_I_Was_God.htm>.

*page 181*     the first camp commandant: Richard Overy, *The Dictators: Hitler's Germany, Stalin's Russia* (New York: W. W. Norton, 2004), p. 601.

*page 182*     "I was raised Episcopalian": *Parade Magazine*, interview with Dan Brown regarding the release of *The Lost Symbol*, September 13, 2009.

*page 186*     "To believe is to be 'in one mind'": Guinness, *In Two Minds*, pp. 24-25.

*page 186*     "You are either kidding yourself": Frederick Buechner, *Wishful Thinking* (New York: Harper & Row, 1973), p. 20.

*page 191*     God is the friend: Kenneth L. Barker and Waylon Bailey, *Micah, Nahum, Habakkuk, Zephaniah*, The New American Commentary, vol. 40 (Nashville: Broadman and Holman, 1999), p. 277.

*page 191*     Guards were trained in a wide range: Overy, *Dictators*, p. 621.

*page 191*     A favorite was the *Pfahlbaum* torture: Ibid., p. 630.

*page 191*     "hop on one foot": Richard J. Evans, *The Third Reich in Power, 1933–1939* (New York: Penguin, 2005), p. 232.

*page 192*     Along with a young pastor: Eric Metaxas, *Bonhoeffer: Pastor, Martyr, Prophet, Spy* (Nashville: Thomas Nelson, 2010), p. 177.

*page 192*     "Suffering is the most acute": Guinness, *In Two Minds*, p. 263.

*page 192*     "First they took the Communists": Evans, *Third Reich in Power*, p. 232.

*page 193*     "In view of his patient suffering": Ibid., p. 231.

**Afterword**

*page 194*     told them to "go far": David McCullough, *Brave Companions: Portraits in History* (New York: Touchstone, 1992), pp. 220-25.